HOW TO CREATE YOUR OWN UNIT STUDY

By Valerie Bendt

Common Sense Press

Other books by Valerie Bendt:

The Unit Study Idea Book
Creating Books With Children
The Frances Study Guide
Success With Unit Studies
For the Love of Reading

Cover photo courtesy of *The Image Bank*

Title page design by Michelle Bendt, age 11

Copyright © 1990. 2nd Revision 1994.
Valerie Bendt

Common Sense Press

P.O. Box 1365
8786 Highway 21
Melrose, FL 32666

ISBN 1-880892-42-1

How To Create
Your Own
Unit Study

CONTENTS

FOREWORD

If you're interested in this book, you have probably already spent time analyzing what is truly valuable in education. You've asked yourself, what is really important, and how can I give my child the best? After all, isn't it for their good that we have taken on this responsibility?

The key to finding direction in all of life is knowing our God-given responsibilities. In regard to children, we are told to "train up a child in the way he should go." Truth, therefore, becomes the major emphasis with academics taking on a lesser role.

If we're going to successfully bake a loaf of bread, we need the right proportion of ingredients, flour being the major foundation, with other necessary ingredients in smaller portions. Likewise, without giving our children a foundation of truth on which to build other learning, their education is not a success no matter how high the test scores.

Our society is trying to function with the belief that education in academics is the solution for all ills. Teaching academics only for success is like trying to make bread using only yeast. It can't be done.

Why is it we can readily recognize proportion and order in other areas of life, but somehow we have been deceived in the area of education?

One of the most difficult tasks in homeschooling is breaking away from the idea that we must teach just like the schools. This belief puts great pressure and guilt on us when we search for a more sensible approach to teaching.

In this book, Valerie has developed a framework for us to break away from school and get involved in life-training using academics to assist us in building that foundation of truth.

Kathleen Ann Albert

All Scripture is inspired by God and profitable for teaching, for reproof, for correction, for training in righteousness; that the man of God may be adequate, equipped for every good work.
2 Timothy 3:16 (NASV)

Kathy is the editor of a local support group news-letter, *The Home Educator's Exchange.* For information, write to: 215 W. Hiawatha, Tampa, FL 33604.

INTRODUCTION

This book was written to encourage you to create studies to strengthen your family. You are your family's best curriculum specialist. You can devise studies superior to any curriculum on the market.

I urge you to put away the tedious texts and delve into real, living books. Sharing good books with your family is rewarding. Involve your children in real-life experiences, providing them with a multitude of pertinent educational encounters. Train them to become self-taught, ensuring a life-long love for acquiring knowledge.

In the margins I have included quotes by key educators, quotes from the Bible and quotes from various classics. Each quote is pertinent to the section in which it is contained. It is my hope that these quotes will spark your interest and cause you to read further. Excerpts from selected classics have been included, as reading good literature is a significant part of our studies.

The wide margins allow you to make notes beside significant passages. An outline is provided to afford you quick reference to desired information.

OUTLINE

I. **Defining Our Goal**
   A. Definition of education taken from Noah Webster's 1828 dictionary contrasted with more current definitions
   B. The purpose of education
   C. Thoughts pertaining to education, by Susan Schaeffer Macaulay

II. **Evaluating Curriculums**
   A. Most curriculums foster a multiple choice mentality
   B. Texts offer bits and pieces of predigested material
   C. Children aren't encouraged to think or reason due to the influence of inferior curriculums
   D. Text and workbook approach stifles creativity

III. **Unit Study Approach**
   A. Major subjects integrated into a particular topic, theme, or historical time period
   B. Studies can be approached biblically
   C. Lesson plans simplified as all ages study one topic
   D. Family unity strengthened
   E. Skills strengthened as each child works at his own level

IV. **Some Educational Philosophies**
   A. Charlotte Mason: 1842-1923
      1. Wrote, among other books, *Home Education*
      2. Chose living books covering a vast range of topics rather than texts
      3. Used time saved in drilling facts to read really good books
      4. Used narration, simply having children retell what had been read
   B. Ruth Beechick
      1. A present-day educator
      2. Uses real books rather than texts
      3. Uses dictation and copying to strengthen skills
      4. Wrote several excellent books including *You Can Teach Your Child Successfully,* and her little books

V. **Phonics and Math**
   A. *Alpha-Phonics*
      1. No need for workbooks
      2. No need for phonetic readers; use the library or have the children dictate their own stories and use them for readers

DEFINING OUR GOAL

The following definitions were taken from the *American Dictionary of the English Language, Noah Webster, 1828.*

> **EDUCATION:** n. The bringing up, as of a child; instruction and discipline which is intended to enlighten the understanding, correct the temper, and form the manners and habits of youth, and fit them for usefulness in their future stations. *To give children a good education in manners, arts and science, is important; to give them religious education is indispensable; and an immense responsibility rests on parents and guardians who neglect these duties!

> **EDUCATE:** vt. To bring up, as a child; to instruct; to inform and enlighten the understanding; to instill into the mind principles of arts, science, morals, religion and behavior. *To educate children well is one of the most important duties of parents and guardians. [2]

The following is a definition taken from the *Webster's Encyclopedia of Dictionaries* — 1978:

> **EDUCATE:** vt. To cultivate and discipline the mind and other faculties by teaching; send to school.[3]

Webster's New World Dictionary — 1988:

> **EDUCATE:** vt. To train or develop the knowledge, skill, mind, or character of, esp. by formal schooling or study; teach; instruct.[4]

There's a tremendous difference between the 1828 Webster's version of education and the definitions we have today. In 1828, education was clearly the responsibility of the parents, and now that responsibility has been given over to the schools. Once parents allowed the schools to take control of the education of their children, it wasn't long before the schools demanded that they have total control. Parents were no longer qualified to oversee their children's education.

It is significant that there is no reference in the Scriptures to the school as a separate institution established by God. In spite of the great importance of the teaching ministry, God has not seen fit to ordain schools as such. Even the implications of the cultural mandate and the Noahic covenant, with the establishment of the institution of human government, do not suggest parallel establishment of schools as instruments of such human governments. As far as the Bible is concerned, the function of transmitting truth and educating the young belongs to the home and church.
—Henry Morris
Christian Education for the Real World, *published by Master Books*

1

You will also notice another sharp contrast between the 1828 definition and the modern definitions of education. In the 1828 version, academics were secondary. A religious education and the child's behavior were deemed most important. Today, the Bible is not even allowed in the public schools. Can character be taught without a basis for truth?

When teaching our children at home, we must ask ourselves, Are we going to reconstruct school at home, or are we going to provide our children with a real education? In her book, *For the Children's Sake,* Susan Schaeffer Macaulay states:

> Education extends to all life. The truly educated person has only had many doors of interest opened. He knows that life will not be long enough to follow everything through fully.[5]

It's our job as parents to introduce our children to a wide variety of interesting topics. We must teach them how to learn so they may further explore areas to which they are drawn.

> The child is not made for education, but education is to serve the child, serve his personality, his life, his needs. — Susan Schaeffer Macaulay.[6]

As we teach our children, we should ask ourselves, Is what I'm teaching really serving my children's needs? Am I filling their minds with tedious, nebulous facts, or am I feeding their minds with the good, the wonderful, the excellent? Enjoy learning and exploring with your children. Learning lasts a lifetime. Scripture gives us that ultimate stick by which to measure all things.

> Finally, brethren, whatsoever things are honest, whatsoever things are just, whatsoever things are pure, whatsoever things are lovely, whatsoever things are of good report; if there be any virtue, if there be any praise, think on these things. Philippians 4:8 (NASV)[7]

EVALUATING CURRICULUMS

Much of the curriculum written for children today fosters the multiple choice or fill-in-the-blank mentality. The children aren't introduced to something as a whole but in bits and pieces of predigested material which they are to regurgitate at the appropriate time. In trying to complete their work, they are looking for the right answers rather than being given the opportunity to grasp a whole concept or idea. Curriculum-driven textbooks and workbooks most often stifle learning and creativity. The use of real or living books allows the children to interact with some very creative and interesting people. These are real authors, not curriculum specialists. Real authors write because they feel they have something valuable to share. Of course, we must still cautiously apply our measuring stick found in Philippians 4:8. There may be parts of books we don't agree with, but we can filter these out or use them to show our children that other people think or act differently than we do. The key here is not to dwell on evil. Our children should know that evil exists, but let's not give them any how-to lessons.

Good books stimulate discussion. If your children can enter into a discussion with you about a book you've read aloud together, then you know they're comprehending. This also helps them to retain a good deal of the material covered. Don't feel you have to process the ideas covered and break them down for the children. Let them try to understand for themselves. This is especially true when reading classics or other great literary works. This will help to stretch their minds. Don't worry about them comprehending every bit of it, but let them take in what's appropriate for them at the time.

True Christian education, as set forth in the Bible, embraces all truth, whether "secular" or "spiritual." It is not narrow and restricted education, as some might assume, but extremely comprehensive—in fact universal—in its scope. Nothing is to be excluded except false knowledge and harmful philosophy, but, unfortunately, these constitute a large component of modern educational curricula. They must be removed from a Christian curriculum, but there is far more than enough genuine and valuable truth to incorporate in their stead.
—Henry Morris
Christian Education for the Real World, *published by Master Books*

I find this a helpful thing to consider as I'm teaching four of my five children together. The younger ones pick up certain things while the older ones pick up more. I try to get them to grasp a whole picture of what's being studied as opposed to isolated facts here and there. These isolated facts mean nothing if there's not a larger framework upon which to build. Sometimes I do find it best in certain areas of study however, to choose simple books that explain things without throwing in a lot of difficult facts. This is true in the area of science.

We studied the human body and I wanted my children to get a feel for the way in which the body systems work together as a whole, before I bombarded them with facts about cells, neurons and protoplasm. They needed to be able to grasp the whole and be acquainted with it before breaking it down into minute parts.

You will find that in technical areas such as science, the simpler books provide the child with an adequate overview of the particular subject being tackled. Few school children are able to recall all the tedious facts drilled into them by their teachers. They get so wrapped up in memorizing these difficult facts that when all's said and done, they don't even have a clear overview of what was being studied.

Sticking with the simpler books in such cases provides the children with enough knowledge to have an understanding of the subject without being overwhelmed and, therefore, totally confused.

We tackled a unit on world geography, but I didn't have the children learn all the countries of the world until they were able to have an understanding of what we mean by "world," "country," and so on. We began with simple library books and branched out from there.

Children can often be introduced to such concepts

through literature. Read a story that takes place in a different country and they begin to get a feel for that country. They realize that it's both similar to and different from their own. Such books can be read on a level above that of your children's reading or comprehension level; this will serve the purpose of stretching their minds while not confusing them with tedious facts to be memorized. They will be introduced to new vocabulary which they will comprehend as the story unfolds. Children can understand many difficult words when used in the context of a story. This is not to be confused with reading them a book with a lot of technical information on which they have no basis to hang this knowledge. There is a big difference between pleasurable reading and technical reading. Technical reading has its proper place after sufficient ground work has been laid.

Biographies are an excellent introduction to different people, ideas, places, and times. While studying our unit on world geography, we read biographies about explorers and missionaries and studied the geographical terms we encountered. Geography became alive through these books.

Let's not recreate the school in the home when we can utilize a superior method of instruction. We don't need to rely on textbooks and workbooks designed to accommodate 30 or 40 children in a classroom. We can use real books, living books that spark our children's interests. You can study history, science, art, music, literature or a host of other subjects by reading biographies about real people in real places, in real space and time. Children prefer this to dry textbooks.

We read twenty biographies in one year. A textbook would possibly donate one or two paragraphs about each of the people we studied. We read

Balboa set off to climb the hill, with Leoncico as his only companion. The journey took him two hours, for he was desperately tired. As he drew near the rocky summit, he realized that he might be approaching the greatest moment of his life. If nothing was visible except more mountains, then his first attempt to find the Southern Sea would have failed. The men were too exhausted to travel much farther without rest and proper food. But if the sea was visible, then he, Vasco Nunez de Balboa, would be the man who had found it. He would be the first European to see the new ocean.

Balboa reached the summit. Eagerly he gazed westward. Far away in the distance lay the Pacific Ocean! Sunshine was sparkling on an expanse of blue water that matched the brightness of the morning sky.

Balboa raised his arm to salute the splendid sight. Now, whatever happened, his name would be remembered in centuries to come. He fell on his knees and began to pray. Far away at the bottom of the hill, seventy Spaniards looked at one another and grinned.
—Balboa, Finder of the Pacific
By Ronald Syme, published by William Morrow and Co.

entire biographies about these people and in turn received a taste of the cultural, economical, political, and geographical climates in which they lived. We were able to experience them as real people, not merely as paragraphs in a textbook. While studying particular units, we are able to see how the lives of certain people overlap. We make figures of each of the people and place them on our timeline. We choose a specific item to go with each person to enable us to better remember them.

Quoting from Charlotte Mason's book entitled *Home Education:*

> The children should have the joy of living in far lands, in other persons, in other times — a delightful double existence; and this joy they will find, for the most part, in their story-books. Their lessons, too, history and geography, should cultivate their conceptive powers. If the child do not live in the times of his history lesson, be not at home in the climes his geography book describes, why, these lessons will fail of their purpose.[8]

You must be wondering, how do I know which books are best, and where do I find them? How do I know I'm teaching all that I should and that there won't be any gaps in my child's education?

Well, life does not afford us enough time to fill in the possible gaps. The only gap to be concerned with is any void in your child's life that can only be filled by the Holy Spirit. Remember, academics aren't everything.

Expose your children to the best in music, art, history, science, and literature. This can be done through the use of living books, real artwork, games, tapes, and so on. Put away the tedious workbooks that inhibit your child from experiencing real life. We form intimate relationships through literature with other people, historical events, and places. As Susan Schaeffer Macaulay states in her book, *For the Children's Sake,* "In literature, perhaps more than through any other art form, we are able to get into the other man's shoes."[9]

These relationships are formed as you share books with your children. A good deal of your school time should be spent reading together. To have time to accomplish this, you must eliminate the unnecessary busy work. It is difficult because we equate learning with filling in countless workbook pages or answering questions at the end of tedious textbook chapters. In order to partake of the excellent, we must throw out what the curriculum specialists have deemed as good.

Suppose I had a room full of parents and I divided it down the middle. Then I informed those on my right that they must complete five workbook pages dealing with reading comprehension, involving reading isolated paragraphs and answering teacher contrived questions. Meanwhile, those on my left would listen to me read several chapters from a really good book about some interesting person, about whom we would afterwards discuss. But before we did this, I would allow anyone to change sides of the room. How many do you think would choose the workbook side? The discussion side? Which side do you think your children would choose? More importantly, which situation is more conducive to learning? Which lesson would be more cost efficient; the one involving a consumable workbook or the one involving a library book or a book of your own which can be used again and again? Let's not have the children equate education with being bored!

Susan Schaeffer Macaulay's book, *For the Children's Sake,* has two companion volumes, which I find to be a tremendous aid in formulating my own curriculum, *Teaching Children, A Curriculum Guide to What Children Need to Know at Each Level Through Sixth Grade;* and *Books Children Love, A Guide to the Best Children's Literature.*

These books are categorized by subject and grade level, which makes them very easy to use. Another useful guide, highly recommended by Mary Pride, is entitled **The Home Schooler's Complete Reference Guide,** for grades K-6. Be flexible when using any book as a guide. Remember, your children are unique and you understand them better than anyone. Follow your instincts.

Next, we will define the term *unit study* and see why it's a more simple and effective way to teach. Along with the unit study approach, I combine the educational practices of both Charlotte Mason and Ruth Beechick.

UNIT STUDY APPROACH

Basic school subjects are studied in light of a particular topic, theme, or historical time period instead of studying eight or more isolated subjects.

Children are able to grasp the wholeness of truth as they see how these subjects relate to one another. Studies are approached from a biblical philosophy of education. Lesson planning is simplified because all ages study a topic together. Families are strengthened through this unity. Field trips, projects, and games all center around a particular unit.

Basic skills are taught in an informal manner while engaged in the study of a particular unit. Previously learned skills are strengthened as the children work at their own level.

SOME EDUCATIONAL PHILOSOPHIES

Let me introduce Charlotte Mason. She lived from 1842 to 1923 and was a teacher, author, and lecturer in England. Her own writings have recently been reprinted; her book, **Home Education,** has a wealth of knowledge for us as parents. She believed in respecting children as whole persons. She believed children should be involved in real life situations, learn self-discipline, and be given ample time for free play.

Studies were limited to the morning hours with afternoons free for creativity and play. The evening hours were to be spent enjoying a good book with the family. She chose to use living books covering a wide range of topics instead of textbooks. She utilized the time saved in drilling facts in a textbook to read really good books. Charlotte Mason didn't believe in pressuring a child into a specific grade level. She stated that this would diminish his assurance of his self-worth. She allowed the child to progress at his own rate while exposing him to the best. I quote Miss Mason:

> This horse-in-a-mill round of geography and French, history and sums, was no more than playing at education; for who remembers the scraps of knowledge he labored over as a child? and would not the application of a few hours in later life effect more than a year's drudgery at any one subject in childhood?[10]

She believed in giving the child a liberal education, introducing him to good books and protecting him from "twaddle." Twaddle was her own word for the worthless, inferior material published for children. She saw that it underrated the child's intelligence. Miss Mason had her students narrate books which had been read aloud. Later, as they matured, this narration would be written. This is reading comprehension fully exercised.

A child who learns early on to narrate orally will be less apt when he is older to encounter the typical problems often associated with written narration. Narration is simply a retelling of what has been read. You know a child is comprehending the material and his retention of that material will be greater when he can express himself in oral narration.

Ruth Beechick, a truly great author and educator of our present day, has also seen the value in using

In saying that EDUCATION IS A LIFE, the need of intellectual and moral as well as of physical sustenance is implied. The mind feeds on ideas, and therefore children should have a generous curriculum.
— Charlotte Mason
Home Education, *published by Tyndale House Publishers*

9

real books rather than textbooks. In her three little books, she instructs parents how to use a natural method in teaching preschool through third grade. One book deals with arithmetic, one with language, and one with reading. She dispenses with complicated teaching methods in favor of simpler and more practical methods. She has also written a number of other books including an excellent one entitled, **You Can Teach Your Child Successfully.** In this book she gives loads of helpful instructions on how to teach using real books instead of texts or workbooks.

Quoting from her book, **You Can Teach Your Child Successfully**:

> Some educators question whether textbooks, even at their best, could ever do the job. 'The very nature of textbooks is to present information that is predigested, prethought, preanalyzed, and presynthesized,' says a school learning specialist. A steady diet of such books deprives children of the joy of original thought. It turns them off to learning![1]

Ruth Beechick explains that although textbook series publishers boast about strengthening concepts, basic skills and generalizations from one grade to the next, these things are not accomplished. The texts are a compilation of separate, disjointed topics.

She stresses the use of dictation as a significantly successful means of teaching. Copying selected passages is useful to younger children and can also be useful to any children who find dictation too difficult. Lessons using copying or dictation integrate writing, grammar, spelling, punctuation, vocabulary, and comprehension skills for a well-balanced educational program.

Dictate a paragraph to your child, observe what he has trouble with and work on that. A grammar handbook will prove to be a beneficial resource. **Learning Grammar Through Writing** is a good book to start with for the lower grades. For the upper elementary grades and high school, I recommend *A Composition Handbook* from Longman. Common Sense Press publishes a book entitled, *Learning Language Arts through Literature,* which implements the copying and dictating learning approach set forth by Ruth Beechick. It gives step-by-step instructions on how to get the full benefit of this method. The selections to be dictated or copied are chosen for you. It has been edited by Ruth Beechick. This will be helpful for those of you new to the dictation method of instruction.

As I use the unit study approach, I incorporate the dictating and copying methods whether we're conducting a literature unit, science unit or whatever. Because all of our studies center on a particular topic, theme or time period, the dictating and copying methods are a very easy way to integrate language arts into any study area. Charlotte Mason's narration method of study is also easily incorporated into a unit study.

There are many other experts in the homeschooling arena advocating a more practical approach to learning as opposed to a textbook-workbook oriented approach. I have read a number of books by these people, but space does not permit me to comment on all of them. Raymond and Dorothy Moore have written numerous books expelling the myth that seeks to legitimize the effectiveness of the workbook approach. As a result of increased awareness, several publishers have produced curriculums based on the unit study method.

I have used or examined some of these curriculums. Although they are superior to the basic workbook-oriented curriculums, I still felt in bondage when using them.

My family's particular needs and desires drive me to develop our own unit studies. It does take time and dedication. But so does trying to keep up with several children working at different levels, on different subjects, in different books. We are learning as a family. Our goals and priorities are based on our needs; they aren't based on someone else's lesson plans, someone who never even met my family.

Next, we will discuss how you can successfully create your own unit studies. Don't let the self-proclaimed experts intimidate you. What was accepted as educationally sound a few years ago is now regarded as incorrect. Why? Because the experts are realizing that their inferior teaching methods and materials don't work. The curriculum specialists plod away trying to come up with new and better methods and materials, and the textbook publishers happily print and sell more new texts and workbooks each year. Have you ever gone to a public school book depository and wondered why they were getting rid of so many books? If the public school doesn't want them, I certainly don't! Let's be cautious of some Christian textbook publishers who mimic the secular, but throw in a Bible verse here and there as a peace offering. This is an insult to true Christianity.

I'd like to quote Ruth Beechick from her book, *You Can Teach Your Child Successfully*:

> For some children and for some time, certain books will happen to be just right. But if you find yourself struggling to mold your child to a book, try reversing priorities. It's the child you are teaching, not the book. Bend the book or find another; make the studies fit the child![12]

PHONICS AND MATH

Before we dive into the *how* of creating your own unit studies, I would like to review some simple and effective programs for teaching phonics and math to younger children. These are also helpful for those needing remedial work.

I am very much impressed with Samuel

Blumenfeld's **Alpha-Phonics.** This is a very sound and easy-to-use phonics program. You don't need workbooks or beginning phonetic readers to use this manual. The print is in large italics, and there are step-by-step instructions for the parent. Most children do well using this simple, no-frills approach. Some phonics programs get so detailed that the student becomes confused. Too many rules often complicate matters. Generally, most any phonics program will do, but you will do well to eliminate much of the workbook tedium. Here again, dictation and copying work well when teaching phonics. You need only spend ten to fifteen minutes several days each week to teach phonics.

Read often to your children. Point out letters or combinations of letters and the sounds they make as you read along. Keep this brief so as not to put a damper on story time. Read using your finger as you go along so your children will become accustomed to reading from left to right. Point out parts of books, such as the table of contents, index, glossary, copyright, author, and illustrator. Read the book jacket, if it includes information about the author and illustrator. Books come alive as you become familiar with their features. The more you read to your children, the more they will want to read for themselves. Continue to read aloud to them even when they become proficient readers. Begin reading to your children when they are very young as this helps to build their attention spans.

It's not necessary to buy very controlled phonetic readers. I was using some with my son, Robert, who was almost six at the time. He was dutifully reading one when he remarked, "Mommy, people don't really talk like that!" I asked him if he would rather write his own books, and he agreed that would be much better. I brought out some large newsprint paper with big lines. I told him to dictate a story to me

The first period—from colonial times to the 1840's—saw the dominance of the Calvinist ethic: God's omnipotent sovereignty was the central reality of man's existence. In the Calvinist scheme, the purpose of man's life was to glorify God, and the attainment of Biblical literacy was considered the overriding spiritual and moral function of education. Latin, Greek and Hebrew were studied because they were original languages of the Bible and of theological literature. Thus, this period in American education is characterized by a very high standard of literacy.
—Samuel Blumenfeld *"Who Killed Excellence,"* published by Imprimis, *1985*

To the memory of my mother: wise in counsel, tender in judgment and in all charity, strong in Christian faith and purpose, I dedicate, with reverence, this simple book.
—*Author's dedication to* The Five Little Peppers and How They Grew *by Margaret Sidney, published by Grosset and Dunlap, Inc.*

"Peter, I know something," she called to him.

"Say it," he replied.

"You must learn to read," was the news she had for him.

"It's no use," was the reply.

"O Peter! I don't agree with you," said Heidi eagerly. "I think that you can after a little while."

"Cannot," remarked Peter.

"Nobody believes such a thing as that, and I don't either," said Heidi very decidedly, "The grandmamma in Frankfurt knew that it wasn't true, and she told me that I ought not to believe it either."

Peter was astonished at this news.

"I will teach you to read; I know how very well," Heidi continued. "You must learn now once for all, and then you must read one or two hymns every day to your grandmother."

—Heidi

By Johanna Spyri, published by Grosset and Dunlap, Inc.

and I would write it down. He came up with many truly creative stories. Afterward, I would have him read the stories back to me. I was fearful that the vocabulary would be too difficult for him, but to my surprise I only had to help him occasionally. His familiarity with his own story enabled him to coast over the more difficult words. I continued to give him more phonics instruction for brief periods, and within six months he had progressed from reading on a kindergarten level to reading on the third grade level. His self-confidence was tremendously boosted and he became quite a good storyteller. His younger brother, Raymond, did not want to be left out, and although he could only read a few short vowel words, he also wanted to dictate stories. I would read his stories back to him. He was so pleased with himself, and I often had to force him to end his stories as his imagination did not want to quit. Now when I ask my boys to write a story, they aren't overwhelmed because they've had so much practice. This method also works well with older children who are reluctant writers.

I like to play games with my children to increase their reading ability. Sometimes I send them on a treasure hunt. First, I give them a note with directions for locating the next note which I have hidden. They continue from note to note until they find the treasure, usually a cookie or some such treat. Sometimes I write them notes at night and leave them in their room for them to discover the next morning. You can make mail boxes for them to keep in their room for these special notes.

Library books are great for beginning readers. The library is loaded with easy readers. Mary Pride advocates the use of Dr. Seuss books as beginning readers. These are easily found in even the most meager of libraries. Let your children choose from several you select. Allow them plenty of time to read at an easy level so they become comfortable with books. Let them continue to choose some easy books even when they are beyond this level. This can be just for fun. Have them dictate stories to you, and if they're comfortable enough, they can write down short stories for themselves. Perhaps they may want to only write a sentence or two and dictate the rest to you or an older sibling. Don't worry about technicalities or spelling at first. Just give lots of encouragement.

If a child doesn't seem to be picking up the phonics, let it rest for a while and continue to read excellent books to him. A child should never be deprived of the benefits of good literature because he cannot read well. Read to him. This is a must for older children as well, who may not read proficiently.

I normally use a math text during our unit study schedule for the older children and a math manual for the younger children. We also play a variety of math games. It is not always possible to integrate math into your unit studies enough to provide sufficient practice in the appropriate areas. I feel that the Saxon Publishing Company markets the best math curriculum for the upper grades, 4th through 12th. I find that hands-on math is best for grades K-3rd. For K-3rd I use a hundred-board with removable number tags, which comes with a manual published by Eunice Coleman. Mrs. Coleman gives directions for making this lovely wooden hundred-board as well as providing number tags, cup hooks, and a manual with worksheets that directly relate to the use of the hundred-board. I have more recently discovered how wonderfully Cuisenaire Rods are used to teach mathematical concepts. These rods can be used with a host of reusable workbooks designed for grades through high school level.

Nat was still working on surveying when he got his first glimpse at an algebra book. That night, for the first time, he studied all night. The sky was paling in the east when he started another notebook: ALGEBRA AND MATHEMATICS: Nathaniel Bowditch His Book.

Every time he had a chance he borrowed the algebra book, to copy it into his note-book. Between times, he copied everything on mathematics he could find in the Cyclopaedia. *Then he studied everything he could find on astronomy over again.*

He was sixteen the summer he figured how to make an almanac.
—Carry On, Mr. Bowditch
By Jean Lee Latham, published by Houghton Mifflin Company

Using a manual or a text is necessary when studying math because it is important to follow a sequential order. But it is extremely important that we don't just teach our children how to do math; they need the concepts behind the figures. Share math with your children in your everyday affairs. Help them to see the importance of using math in real life. There are a number of adequate math curriculums available. You should find one that suits your needs.

SCHEDULES AND ROUTINES

My method and schedule for conducting unit studies may not be suited to you and your family. I am trying to emphasize that you can devise a program that will be right for your family, that can be superior to anything else on the market, because you know your children better than anyone else except our Lord. Earnestly pray and He will give you the guidance you need.

Please, don't assume that other home educators have it all together and never experience failure. This just isn't true. Neither is it true for the classroom teacher. You will grow as a home educator only when you are willing to jump in with both feet. Experience will be your best teacher. What may work with some families might not work with yours. Dare to be different. Our Heavenly Father created us all with unique abilities and tastes. If we were all the same, we'd find life very monotonous. You can gain a great deal from other home educators, but you must first temper it with biblical truth and then rely on your intuition. I can't begin to tell you the number of plans and curriculums I've tried over the years. A fair amount of selection is trial and error, but if we can push aside the world's false view of education, we'll be on the road to a happy home-education experience.

Reading has helped open my eyes in the area of education. I may not agree with every point that every author brings forth, but I'm now able to sort out what's good for my family from what isn't. There's a fine balance to be had between structure and freedom. We should never get so far from the middle that we lose sight of either end. We do need to be able to lean to one side or the other.

Just as our Heavenly Father has given us laws to govern our lives, He has also given us much freedom within those boundaries. Some people have gone too much one way, leading to legalism, while others have gone too far the other way, leading to licentiousness or a free-for-all life style.

Homeschooling requires a schedule, maintained while remaining flexible. When we were immersed in our world geography unit, my children were writing about the countries in South America as I was dictating to them. I said to my girls, "Today I am going to dictate to you about Brazil." Then they both blurted out, "Oh, please let's do Chile today instead!" I was able to be flexible enough to agree to that, since it didn't alter my ultimate goal. If they had asked to cancel school that day instead of taking dictation on Brazil, I'm sure I would have responded quite differently!

We must learn to be patient with our children, not pushing them to the point of being stressed out, while encouraging them to do their best and not be lazy. As my father once commented, it takes a quiet determination to educate your children. Education is a discipline. We must set a good example for our children in this area.

Children perform best when they have a set routine. This is an area where fathers can help out. Although I do the majority of the teaching, my husband gets the children up at six o'clock each

"Schedule" is a bad word to some people. Perhaps school bells and other regimentation have created aversion toward the idea. The real question is whether we are willing to work in harmony with the natural law or against it. We and our children function more efficiently when we are working closely with our body cycles. In order to make the most of our children's health, security, disposition, and discipline, it is vital that their meals and times for bed, naps, and baths be regular and consistent within reason. This is also basic for any smoothly run household.
—Raymond and Dorothy Moore
Home Style Teaching, published by Word Books Publisher

weekday morning, gets them breakfast (generally cold cereal), has a breakfast Bible study with them and helps them get started on their chores before he leaves for work. All this while I'm dragging myself out of bed, showering and dressing. Then I get something to eat, and by the time I'm finished eating they are dressed and ready to begin their school work. School goes very smoothly when we begin and end early, and my husband can spend time with the children before he leaves for work. It's amazing how good their attitudes are when we keep this schedule. My husband is the key factor for setting the tone for the day.

It is important for husbands and wives to sit down together and decide what sort of schedule should be arranged for their school day. They should decide what forms of discipline should be used for laziness, disobedience and so forth. Then, the children should be made aware or these rules and the consequences of not following them. If a child thinks he can wear down Mom and therefore not have to do his work or at least not all of it, then he will do just that. Mom will be burned out in a very short time. As difficult as it may sometimes be, Mom must not give in to the manipulating child. Here Dad can relieve Mom of some of the mental stress of dealing with disruptive attitudes. Often these attitudes can be squelched if Dad spends only a few minutes with his children in the mornings before school. He can let them know that he wants to see what they have accomplished when he gets home from work. This doesn't necessarily have to be done in a negative way, but even so, it makes them accountable for their behavior and school work. Then the children will actually look foward to showing Dad all they've done during the day.

You have undoubtably read about or come across mothers who teach all their children together at the same time. They may be teaching several children, all at the dining room table, all working out of different books, all working on different subjects all at the same time! Somehow they manage. But that's just it, they are managers and not necessarily teachers.

I find that using the same unit study for all my children works best. They each work at an appropriate level, while we all still maintain a sense of oneness. Even while utilizing this study method, I find it best not to try to always work with all my children at the same time. The baby plays during the first part of our school time and naps during the second part. Generally, I begin by working with the four older children as a group, then I allow the two younger boys to go and play quietly while I work with my two older girls. After I've finished studies with the girls, they read silently or attend to a project, thus enabling me to give more individualized attention to my boys. I find it helpful to pair them in this way. We actually accomplish more than if I tried to continuously work with them all. It makes for much less competition and confusion. However, because we are all studying the same unit, the synergy of the unit is preserved and my preparation time is shortened. You must experiment to see what works best for your family.

When approaching a unit, it's often helpful to do an overview. Then you can temporarily drop the unit and come back to it at a later date and focus on some of its finer details. When we studied our unit on world geography, for instance, there was no realistic way to study each and every country in depth. But because we learned many geographical terms and the locations of all the countries, we will be able to conduct a mini-unit pertaining to one or more countries at a future date. The main world geography unit gave the children an overview of the world, while the mini-unit zeros in on a specific location in the world.

This holds true for our unit on the human body. We did an overview of the body and its systems and learned the names of the organs and bones. I chose to study the eye, the bones and the stomach in more depth. We read two biographies, one of a scientist and one of a physician. Later we will go back and study the other organs in more depth. Now they have some general information about the body on which to hang the information they will be exposed to in the future.

How much time should be spent on each unit? This should be left at your discretion because you know your own family's needs and abilities. Many people ask this question, so I will share with you a plan related to me by another homeschooling mom at one of my workshops.

We begin by taking off two weeks, during which time I plan two units to be covered during the following ten-week period. This two-week break enables the children and me to sew, make crafts, bake, or work on any other projects that seem to get pushed aside. In the midst of this two-week break, I go to the library by myself so I can concentrate entirely on the units to be studied. I break the ten-week period into two five-week units to prevent me from going overboard on a unit. I plan my units in such a way that the more complicated unit comes first. If I find I need additional time, I borrow it from the next five-week period. I select something light and enjoyable for the second five-week unit, particularly something that allows us to get out of doors a good deal. (Remember, you can read outside under the shade of a big tree, and the toddlers can play in the grass and still absorb much information.) This is also a good time to conduct a unit that is primarily project oriented, affording the children more enjoyment because there is less academic emphasis.

By implementing this two-week-off and ten-week-on schedule, we complete four 10-week periods and five 2-week periods. In the course of a year, a two-week period remains and can be inserted at any time into my schedule, such as holiday times or vacations. This routine allows me to teach for 200 days out of the year, while the public schools conduct classes for only 180 days.

Taking off three months during the summer only complicates matters as you lose the discipline of schooling, and afterwards you must review rusty skills. My children really look forward to their two-week vacation, and they plan ahead the projects they want to undertake. During this two-week period there's none of the "Mommy, I'm bored" because they have so much free time on their hands. They know their time is limited so they make the best of it. Each family is different so you should find a plan that works for you.

We previously homeschooled all year round, and I never seemed to have any time for myself. I was always trying to squeeze my lesson plans into any available slot. Now, I'm much more content. I also find a book to read on homeschooling to help give me fresh ideas and motivate me to keep on.

Over the course of the months that I've taken to write this book, my own schedule has been altered to meet the needs of my family. It's wonderful how homeschooling allows us the flexibility we need to remain close.

GETTING STARTED

Beginning your unit study is as simple as picking a topic. You can choose any topic that interests you and your family. If you're worried about covering all the necessary material covered in a regular school curriculum, use *Teaching Children* or *The Home Schooler's Complete Reference Guide* as a basic framework. As I mentioned before, I'm not too worried about what others say we should be teaching our children or when they say we should be teaching these things. Remember, you are teaching the children, not the book.

I'm often asked about the effectiveness of using unit studies when teaching high-school students. I believe this is definitely the best method for instructing older children as well and provides you with an opportunity to guide them in meaningful research. You are actually teaching them how to learn. You have an opportunity to show them how you put together a unit of study, and you are giving them the tools to go on and learn for themselves. After you have given them sufficient instruction in putting together a unit study, you can have them pick a topic and research it on their own, and they can lead the rest of the family through this unit study. This teaches them about a particular topic, and they are simultaneously learning research and teaching skills. After all, we want our children to go on to teach their children at home.

This unit study conducted by your high-school students can be as brief or as elaborate as suits their abilities and needs. It also provides a good opportunity to research careers, maybe even spur them on to starting their own businesses. The possibilities here are endless.

Many may be concerned about teaching all the

subjects ordinarily taught in high school. There are several approaches. One is to use textbooks (which can be obtained free of charge at certain times during the year from the public school book depository) and use them as a general guide. Be cautious and only use the table of contents, chapter outlines, summaries and/or glossaries. You can get a general feel for what's being covered and at what time for each subject. Some curriculum publishers make scope and sequence charts available free of charge, which are useful as guides. (When a scope and sequence chart states that a particular topic is covered, it may mean that only an introduction to this topic is given. You may notice this particular topic is covered again the next year, as is often the case.)

Cathy Duffy's *Christian Home Educators' Curriculum Manual, Junior/Senior High* is the most comprehensive resource I have found for devising high-school studies. Cathy indicates the usual subject matter covered in each grade and has many reproducible charts for keeping records to benefit the college-bound student. (She also has a manual for the elementary grades.) With a minimal amount of research, you can plan the unit studies for your high-school student for the year.

Some topics we have chosen for our unit studies have been: sculpture, four composers studied simultaneously, three American poets studied simultaneously, architecture, famous painters, the writing of the United States Constitution, the instruments of the orchestra, sound, the Tabernacle, world geography and explorers, the human body, and children's authors, along with writing our own books. We plan to study more poets, artists, composers, geometry and famous mathematicians, astronomy, early America, flowers, butterflies, insects, trees, and Florida history, just to name a few. Sometimes, while in the midst of one study, our interests are sparked on to another related topic. Some teachers might call this being side-tracked; I call it opportunity.

You can make your unit study brief or in depth. You can even decide as you progress through a unit just how much material you want to cover. Children do better if they first get an overall, basic level picture of what you're studying. You can then proceed to more closely cover the fine points. You should be striving for real learning, not just fact memorization. When choosing a topic, be sure to pick one that will enable you to locate sufficient materials from the library. If you pick a topic that is too highly specialized, you may not find many resources. On the other hand, if you pick a topic that is too general, you may find the study to be never-ending. You need some limitations. When we did our unit on world geography, I began to realize that we could go on forever. I then made a basic outline of the material I wanted to cover. I deviated from this basic outline somewhat as we progressed, but it prevented me from going to extremes. I realized we just couldn't cover everything, so we hit what I felt were the main points. We can explore the other areas in more detail by planning mini-units covering various countries or geographical land formations. The topics for units based on a geography study are endless.

Some encyclopedias have outlines accompanying their various articles that you can use as a basic guide for your particular unit study. Try to think of other areas of interest you can tie into your basic topic. For instance, when we studied world geography, we studied the lives of seven early explorers and one female missionary. We read complete biographies of each of these people.

For each unit study I locate biographies of those whose lives relate to our particular topic. My older children and I take turns daily reading aloud from these biographies while my younger children listen. This gives practice with oral reading as well as listening skills. A biography is an excellent tool enabling our children to experience the cultural, economical, geographical and political climate of a time and place. This encompasses actual social studies. We are learning about real people in real times in real places, not abstract data.

Use maps frequently so you and your children will become familiar with the places people lived. You can discuss how they talked, what they ate, what they wore, what they believed in, what they did for entertainment, and so on. Children are far more interested in these things than in dry, textbook data.

I commented previously that for each biography read, my children and I make a figure representing that person to go on our timeline. We discuss what particular things about that person stand out foremost in their minds. For instance, when we studied various American poets, we read a biography about Robert Frost, and my daughter drew him with blue eyes and tennis shoes, and holding a piece of paper in his hand with the title of his well-loved poem, "Stopping by Woods on a Snowy Evening." Those things stuck in her mind. We cover these timeline figures with clear contact paper for durability.

Many people like the idea of using a timeline but do not have the wall space. I will offer another alternative. We decided to remove our timeline even though we have the wall space, because it didn't seem very effective. A ladder was needed to reach the top! I didn't feel my children were truly able to benefit from it as well as something they could hold in their hands. Consequently, we have switched to a 14" x 17" binder with plastic sleeves purchased from an art and drafting supply store. We cut poster board on which we draw three lines horizontally,

For children, timelines are not for pulling together the scattered pieces of knowledge, as they do so well for adults; children haven't yet collected enough pieces to pull together. What timelines can do for children is to provide a framework into which they can put pieces of knowledge as they learn them.
— Ruth Beechick
You Can Teach Your Child Successfully,
published by Arrow Press

one half inch wide and four inches apart, representing our timelines. As the portfolio opens, the lines continue across the two pages and, for example, represent the 1700's. We use different pages to represent different time periods, and where necessary, several pages represent a particular time period. When few individuals from a time period are likely to be studied, several hundreds of years are represented on one or two pages.

We cut 3″ x 5″ index cards in half, and the children draw their historical figure on the card. The children then add distinguishing features indicative of their historical figure, including the individual's name and birth and death dates at the bottom of the card. Using a card of a specific size helps us to maintain a uniformity in our portfolio, but the children are allowed to represent their figure in any fashion they choose on the card. The timeline-figure cards are inserted into pre-cut slits made on the portfolio pages. These slits are made like those in an old-fashioned photo album, allowing the corners of the cards to be tucked into the slits. Each portfolio page holds twelve cards, four across and three down.

Borders around the pages, illustrative of the time period, enhance the timeline portfolio. This is especially useful for the time periods where we have studied few individuals, enabling the children to grasp the flavor of that segment of history. The timeline pages are inserted into the plastic sleeves and easily removed for including additional figures.

A timeline portfolio makes a great hands-on teaching aid for children and still allows your family the flexibility to be creative. Some children want their own timelines, in which case you can use a regular or slightly larger notebook with plastic sleeves. These are available at most office supply stores.

I'm sure there are many of you who feel uneasy

about breaking away from textbooks. It is my belief this anxiety will be relieved as you become more and more frustrated with textbooks. You can experiment with the unit study approach while remaining safe within the pages of your textbooks. Allow me to suggest a simple plan.

Choose one of your children's textbooks, a history text for example. Peruse the textbook until you find a chapter that interests you. Note the key people, places, and events in this chapter and choose relative library books. Generally, I suggest selecting one biography, one or two books pertaining to the place being studied and one or two books relating to a specific event, discovery or invention mentioned in the textbook chapter. (See the library check list in the next section for more information on selecting books.) Do not read the textbook chapter to your children, although you may want to read it yourself. Do not have them answer the questions at the end of the chapter. Have fun with this unit. Determine how much time you will spend on this study (perhaps two or three weeks), and when you have completed the unit study resume your regular textbook studies. Try this approach later in the year, using a chapter from a science text, literature text or other textbook. If you are teaching several children, use a history text from one grade level to conduct a unit and a science text from another grade level for your next unit. Don't use any textbooks other than a math text during your unit study as all other subjects will be integrated into your main topic. You may need to reduce some of your children's workbook or textbook written work during the year to afford you the necessary time to conduct these unit studies. This can be accomplished as you have the children do some of their work orally.

I want to encourage you parents using a published

unit study to tailor the studies to fit your family. Don't feel obligated to cover all the material in the manual. Use the manual as a resource book. Select units that appeal to you and your family. Use only the information that will help you achieve the goals you have for your family. If a particular study spurs your interest in another area, feel free to explore that on your own.

USING THE LIBRARY

You may not always be certain which biographies of famous persons are appropriate for your study. We like to read biographies of several explorers while studying our geography units. I can recall only a few explorers, so I go to the reference section of the children's department of the public library and find several indexes to aid me in my search for materials for my unit study. One such book is the **Index to Collective Biographies for Young Readers: Elementary and Jr. High Level,** compiled by Judith Silverman. I look up explorers and find literally pages of them under subheadings such as French Explorers, Spanish Explorers, etc. These also list the birth and death dates of the explorers. This is helpful as I want to choose explorers predominately from the same time period.

Our studies are enhanced as we read these biographies and begin to see how the lives of these explorers overlap. We find some of them had sailed together or used the knowledge acquired by another's voyage to further their own expeditions. History comes alive as you see how the lives of people intertwine.

We also use that particular index to find the names of American poets. First, I look up poets, and then under that I find the subheading for American poets. This index is also useful for browsing through to find a subject you're interested in studying. Then, under the particular subject you choose, you will find various lists or pertinent names of persons whose biographies you can read. The titles for all of these biographies are listed elsewhere in the book and are located by using the book's cross-reference coding. There is another helpful reference book entitled **People in Books,** by Margaret Nicholsen. This is easier to use than the **Index to Collective Biographies for Young Readers,** because no cross-reference system is used to locate book titles. However, it is not as extensive.

It is not always necessary to use one of these indexes to find biographies, as most are easily found by locating the Junior Biography section of your library and looking under that particular person's last name. The books are shelved in alphabetical order. The indexes are extremely helpful for locating persons who do somehow relate to your study. If your library doesn't have an appropriate biography, the **Index to Collective Biographies for Young Readers,** or **People in Books** will be helpful. Look in these indexes to see if such a biography does exist about a person, or perhaps that person is included in a book that covers several different persons. If you discover an appropriate book, find out if your branch has it in its card catalogue, and if it doesn't, have the librarian check to see if another branch does. Usually it only takes a few days to transfer a book from another branch.

The **subject card catalogue** can also aid in your search for particular books pertaining to your topic, including biographies and other helpful books. When studying geography, I use the subject card catalogue to find books on maps and countries. Finding books will be much simpler after you become acquainted with your library. Often you can go straight to a certain area to find the books you

Young children are very much interested in the world and people around them. If we begin reading biographies and enjoyable historical novels to our children before history has a chance to become a boring subject, we are more likely to create a positive lifelong attitude towards history.
—Cathy Duffy
Christian Home Educator's Curriculum Manual, Elementary Grades, *published by Home Run Enterprises*

Let him on the contrary, linger pleasantly over the history of a single man, a short period until he thinks the thoughts of that man, is at home in the ways of that period. Though he is reading and thinking of the lifetime of a single man, he is really getting intimately acquainted with the history of a whole nation for a whole age.
— Charlotte Mason
Home Education, published by Tyndale House Publishers

want because you've become familiar with the layout of the library.

During your unit study, it's good to use some books that are written on an easy level but that cover key points. Don't be afraid to use books which are on an advanced reading level, even books from the adult section of the library, as many of these books have excellent pictures. This is especially true of the fine art section. You may choose to read various selections from these books to your children or use them only for their pictures.

Not every book we find will be in harmony with our beliefs. You can either skip undesirable sections of books or use them for discussing your beliefs and how others believe. You can explain to your children that not everything in print is accurate and therefore must be tempered with Scripture.

You will find many helpful guides and reference manuals in the children's reference section of your public library; some of these we reviewed earlier. Many of the children's classics are also found in the reference section. These may not be checked out, but they often have copies which may be checked out on the regular book shelves. Browsing through these classics in the reference section will familiarize you with these timeless books. Other pertinent books are located in the reference section and are usually worth investigating.

Be sure to utilize audio cassette tapes, video tapes and art work which can all be checked out and will enhance your unit study. Remember to keep things simple at first.

The following check list may assist you in your search for materials to be obtained from the library. This list suggests major areas from which to choose materials, depending on the unit.

Biographies: Select biographies of those persons

relating to your unit of study. (Remember, the reference section is helpful for this.)

Non-fiction: Choose factual books pertaining to your unit, i.e., books on the solar system, the Revolutionary War, famous inventions, etc.

Fiction: These include stories relating by topic or time period to your unit. There are many interesting historical novels, animal stories, and so on.

Easy Books: Find both easy readers and simple books that accentuate key points.

Fine Art: Investigate the children's section and the adult section. For instance, if you're studying boats, look for books with reproductions of boats. The fine arts section has a subject catalogue that makes this an easy task. Many libraries have framed art reproductions that can be checked out. Biographies and works of artists are also available. You will discover books pertaining to architecture in this section to enhance the study of a particular place or time period.

Music: Locate audio cassette tapes, records and song books relating to your unit by style or topic. Also examine composers or artists of the same time period.

Arts and Crafts: Select arts and crafts books representative of your topic or time period. There are several historically based craft books. (Example: *Let's Be Early Settlers with Daniel Boone.*)

Literature and Poetry: Investigate famous poets and authors of the same time period and location as your study or who wrote about the topic you are covering. Investigate poems and plays relating to your topic. Plays may be either read aloud or acted out in costume.

Home Economics: Cookbooks are great tools for studying particular historical time periods or the cultures of various countries. (Example: *The Little House Cookbook.*)

Clothing: There are several interesting books that depict the costumes of particular time periods and various countries or trades.

Videocassettes: Numerous videos are available that pertain to foreign countries, artists' lives and works, storytelling, science experiments, foreign languages, and sign language. Classic movies, plays, and ballets are also obtainable on videocassette.

Science: If you are engaged in a unit that's primarily a science unit, you will of course find books in this area. However, science can come into play in historical units as you investigate inventions, inventors, and discoveries of the day. There are many science experiment books that can be integrated into your unit.

Some of the areas mentioned can be incorporated later and used to review material previously covered. This material can be viewed from a different perspective.

(Please refer to the Library Reference Guide at the end of this book for information on the resources available in the children's reference section of your public library.)

Briefly review the library books you have chosen. Find one or two key books to serve as your basic texts, preferably a suitable biography and/or a readable book that covers key points. Books that have an abundance of technical information may be helpful for reference purposes but will not qualify as an overall text. Your text should present a general overview of the material to be covered.

These key books will suffice as material for you to read aloud to your children. This will unite the family in the study, while offering discussion time which stimulates reading comprehension. Each child will benefit as he absorbs that which he is able. Employ the capable children to read portions of these books aloud.

It is helpful to categorize the remaining books into groups by subject, that is, relating to music, art, science, fiction, non-fiction, literature, easy books, and so on. You may use some books only for their illustrations or photographs, others may serve for your children to read on their own, and some books may be beneficial for copy work or dictation. As a suggested activity, have your children read some of these books on their own, making a list of the words they don't understand. These words can be looked up in the dictionary. Occasionally, glossaries are included in factual books. Index cards are helpful as the children write the unknown word on the front and the definition on the back. The cards are useful for later review and can be shared with the other siblings.

You may find some books are repetitious, so choose only those that suit your needs. Allowing older children to read some of the simpler books to the younger children benefits the older as well as the younger. It reinforces what they have been learning, gives them practice reading aloud, helps to form strong bonds between siblings, and prepares for future roles as parent-teachers. (Not to mention, it frees you up a little, too.)

As you become more proficient at conducting unit studies, you learn to weed out books while at the library so you don't come home swamped. Remember, you can always devote more time to a unit at a later date. Don't feel you have to totally exhaust the library and put to use every book it contains on any given subject. (For instance, we conducted an American Revolution unit and viewed that era through the eyes of its painters. At a later date, we will focus on the music of the Revolution.)

USING GAMES AND TEACHING AIDS

I've found that games are a great way for children to learn about various subjects. They are nonconsumable (may be used again and again), and they are good for reviewing previously covered material. Aristoplay makes excellent educational games. We use their game *Where in the World?* when conducting our geography units. My girls and I learn the names and locations of each country in the world and their major seacoasts. We also learn key facts about many of the countries. Even my younger boys benefit from this game. One writing exercise that my children enjoy was inspired by this game. The game has a deck-sized card for each country including that country's name, flag, literacy rate, monetary unit, major languages, major seacoast, major import, and major export. I have my children make up their own country and make a card for it which includes these same items. Then they make a map showing the location of the country, and they write a paragraph about the people of that make-believe country. You will quickly find that it isn't difficult to invent writing assignments or come up with projects relating to your unit study. Let the children think up some assignments themselves; most children can be very creative when given a chance.

Each Aristoplay game has directions for playing several different games on several different levels, increasing its effectiveness.

I like to have an accompanying game for each unit we cover. This offers variety to our study and is a good tool for review. You can also make your own games to fit your study. This of course takes time, but it is also less expensive. My children have always enjoyed the games I have made. Your children can invent games to go along with your unit study; this will cause them to probe for questions and answers pertaining to your unit study. They will use many valuable skills making up their own games, offering a beneficial, occasional change of pace.

For some units, you may want to do a little extra and purchase a few additional items to enhance your study. For instance, our biggest unit we covered one past school year was our world geography unit. Not only did we purchase the **Where in the World?** game, but we bought a map-of-the-world shower curtain. This has proven beneficial to the entire family. I find myself brushing up on my countries while in the shower. To keep pace with the children, this is necessary.

We already had a globe. I bought two tapes from Audio-Memory Publishng Company entitled **Geography Songs** and **More Geography Songs.** We still listen to these tapes to keep ourselves up to date on our geography facts. My dad gave the children a terrific book put out by National Geographic called **Exploring Your World**. It's an alphabetized glossary of geographical terms with beautiful full-color pictures. I use this book to dictate geographical terms to my children. As we read the biographies of various explorers, we encounter certain terms which we look up in **Exploring Your World,** and I dictate the definitions of these terms to the children.

USING DICTATION AND COPYING

I would like to talk more about the benefits of dictation. Many older children do well when passages of pertinent material are dictated to them; however, younger children can copy the selections you choose. When implementing the copying exercises, I neatly write out what I want them to copy so they have a model showing proper letter

We need to change the way most of us think, so that we can see learning opportunities in many things around us. We need to change our "mind set" so that we can see other things than textbooks as curriculum material.
—Cathy Duffy
Christian Home Educators' Curriculum Manual, Elementary Grades, *published by Home Run Enterprises*

formation. Older children may be able to copy directly from a book. As you work with your children you will be able to discern exactly what form of copying or dictation they can do and how much. Start slowly and gradually build up. Don't exhaust them.

As I dictate to my children, or as they copy a selection, I emphasize important points about spelling, punctuation, capitalization, vocabulary, and so forth. When I'm dictating a passage with difficult punctuation, I read in the punctuation and explain the reasoning for its use. Sometimes, I may dictate a sentence and then tell them that there are three commas in that sentence and ask them to put them in. Then I check to see if they have placed them in their proper places. Or, sometimes I put in extra commas and ask them which commas should be removed. For younger children copying a selection, I sometimes omit punctuation in the passage they are to copy and inform them that they need to put in the punctuation. They learn considerably more from these methods of dictation and copying than they would from isolated worksheets dealing with spelling, punctuation, capitalization, vocabulary, etc. They are also working from a model that uses correct grammar and sentence structure. At the same time the children are learning these useful skills, they are learning about the topic we are studying. Valuable time is not wasted in the area of basic skills, but rather is integrated into real learning.

If a child is continuously exposed to well written material, whether by reading, copying, dictating or listening, he will be influenced in a positive way, much more so than by filling in worksheet after worksheet.

Studies indicate that those who learn to diagram sentences well do not automatically become good writers. Those who write well do so because they are

36

exposed to good writing, and they themselves write often. I have a friend who is an author and a former editor who plainly states she couldn't diagram a sentence if her life depended on it. If you go for a job interview, certainly on the application they will not ask you to diagram a sentence; but, they might very well ask for an essay. Sentence diagraming is an effective tool allowing us to see **how** the parts of a sentence interact. It does not show **why**. Dwelling on such tedium is unnecessary; however, an introduction to these inter-relations is a beneficial exercise for your older students. I suggest using the ***Winston Grammar Kit***, as it uses a hands-on approach to sentence diagraming.

Many famous authors used the copying method to train themselves to be proficient writers, just as skillful artists have for centuries copied the works of the great masters. Copying was the self-teaching method of Benjamin Franklin.

You will find in any field of excellence that conscientious people seek out and copy those who are experts. It's actually so simple and works so well that it's difficult for us to believe that it produces sound writers.

We use this method of dictation and copying extensively since it is so beneficial and yet so simple. After choosing the topic for our unit study, we converge on the library, and I select our books while the children busy themselves choosing books of their own interest. As mentioned earlier, I select a biography or several biographies of persons whose lives somehow relate to our unit of study. I also choose books directly relating to the subject matter at hand, choosing both easy and more difficult books.

Before beginning our lessons, I briefly skim these books and choose a selection to read to the children. Generally, I pick the most significant material,

"Now," said Polly, "how'll we do it, Ben?" as they ranged themselves around the table, on which reposed the cakes. "You begin."

"How do folks begin a letter?" asked Ben, in despair, of his mother.

"How did Jasper begin his?" asked Mrs. Pepper back again.

"Oh!" cried Polly running into the bedroom to get the precious missive. " 'Dear Miss Polly'—that's what it says."

—The Five Little Peppers and How They Grew
By Margaret Sidney, published by Grosset and Dunlap, Inc.

sometimes skipping sentences that aren't crucial. However, even those sentences that are skipped are read, but not for the purpose of dictation. Truly undesirable portions are left out altogether. Usually, I will dictate **pertinent information** from an entire book so as to give continuity to our study. Of course, with some books, only certain sections or chapters may pertain to your study, and some books I use for pictures or diagrams only. I also choose simple books that I read to the younger children, and they use these for their copy work. My older children read these books on their own during quiet time; this helps to reinforce our study. Once we have read a biography aloud together, I use the summary of the book found in the front of the book jacket as a dictation or copying exercise for my children. This is an excellent way to capsulize the book. They are being given a good example of a book summary which will aid them in learning to write their own summaries.

How much dictation or copy work should your children do? The answer to this question can only be found as you work with your children. For very young children, one key sentence may be enough. More experienced children may write a paragraph. My two girls have worked up to writing 1 to 2 pages, handwritten on notebook paper from dictation. My boys, who are younger, copy one or two pertinent sentences that I have written for them after having read a book or chapters from a book to them. I select these sentences from those books dealing with our unit of study. For the boys, I use the large, lined newsprint paper purchased from a school supply store. I write the selection to be copied at the top of the paper, paying attention to letter formation and spacing. Then the children have a good model from which to copy.

THE IMPORTANCE OF WRITING

It's very crucial that our children learn to write well. An excellent book, offering much inspiration for teaching children to write, **Write From the Start,** by Donald Graves and Virginia Stuart, is available at the public library. In this book, Mr. Graves makes an interesting statement:

> A well-written piece can transcend the barriers within a society that demands diplomas and other certificates of achievement![13]

The apostle Paul states in the Bible that he could more effectively communicate the Lord's word through the written word than in person. Therefore, he was able to have an effective ministry even while in prison.

Being able to put thoughts into words and thereafter into the written word is a goal we and our children should strive toward. Dictation and copying serve as an effective means of achieving this goal.

Let your children see you reading and writing and, thereby, serve as an example, for children are good imitators. Later, I will discuss the usefulness of incorporating Scripture into dictation or copying exercises...more precisely as typing exercises.

PROJECTS: FRIEND OR FOE?

Most published unit study curriculums are noted for their heavy emphasis on projects. Their contention is that children learn best by doing. While this is generally true, most mothers burn out trying to organize all these activities. These hands-on projects are nice once in a while and add a change of pace to your unit studies, but a steady diet only leads to frustration for Mom.

Don't feel guilty if you hear about other mothers who produce volcanic eruptions on their dining room tables or make relief maps of the world from

Writing is certainly a medium for communication, as all art forms are. It gives the opportunity for direct communication, for verbalizing thoughts and attitudes, for speaking truth and putting content into expression.
— Edith Schaeffer
Hidden Art, *published by Tyndale House Publishers*

We older people, partly because of our maturer intellect, partly because of our defective education, get most of our knowledge through the medium of words. We set the child to learn in the same way, and find him dull and slow. Why? Because it is only with a few words in common use that he associates a definite meaning; all the rest are no more to him than the vocables of a foreign tongue. But set him face to face with a thing, and he is twenty times as quick as you are in knowing all about it; knowledge of things flies to the mind of a child as steel filings to a magnet.
— Charlotte Mason
Home Education, published by Tyndale House Publishers

papier-mâché...done to scale! Tailor your curriculum to fit your family's needs. Don't try to "keep up with the Joneses." One advantage of creating your own curriculum is that if you find a technique or a book doesn't work for you or your children, you have the freedom to alter it. And if you haven't spent hundreds of dollars on a curriculum you are not pleased with, you feel less obligated to continue because of a monetary investment.

I find my children prefer to have access to plenty of paper, markers, paints, fabric scraps, glue, milk cartons and so forth from which to make their own creations. Whether pertaining to our unit studies or not, they are using their creative imaginations; therefore, real learning is taking place. All learning does not have to be adult-contrived.

Children learn about the world around them as they play, observe nature, observe others at play or work, and as they have the freedom to explore and create. Of course, this doesn't mean they are totally unsupervised, but they are given immense freedom within certain boundaries. Some of the best projects we have done relating to our unit studies have been those devised by my children. If you ask your children to devise a project for a particular unit, you will be surprised how creative they can be. I find it helpful when engaged in a project to ease up a great deal on the more academic aspects of our unit and just concentrate on the project.

CHOOSING YOUR UNITS OF STUDY

As I plan my units to be studied, I try to organize them in such a way as to encompass a variety of subjects within the year. One unit may deal predominantly with social studies, such as a unit on world geography, while the next might have its main thrust in science, such as a unit on the human body. A following unit's major theme might be literary, based on the study of children's authors. (During this unit, the children can write and illustrate their own books.) A subsequent unit might have its roots in mathematics and encompass a study of geometry and famous mathematicians of long ago. Afterward, we might study something lighter—like animals or insects—then perhaps music or art. By alternating basic subject studies, we add variety to our curriculum and achieve a well-rounded course of study.

I'm often asked if it is necessary to conduct units as a family, especially if the children have varied interests. I personally enjoy conducting units together as a family because of the closeness it builds and the discipline it instills in my children. As we work together, they learn to respect one another and they have many opportunities to learn patience. However, just having your children home all day allows for this type of interaction to a large degree. If your children are capable of conducting a unit on their own, with a certain amount of input from Mom and Dad, they can share this newfound information with the rest of the family. You might wish to set aside a certain day or evening for this purpose. This in itself would be a good opportunity for the children to improve their oral skills. We've also heard it said many times that the best way to remember something is to teach it to someone else.

Delight is any deep and enduring interest that draws a person to apply his heart and mind to study. Your student's delight can either be harnessed to pull other subjects, or it can be held hostage to other subjects!
—Gregg Harris "Delight Directed Studies," The Teaching Home

It would be wise for each of us to allow our children to pursue individual units at some point to strengthen additional skills. This is definitely a desirable method for older children. We should be teaching them to teach themselves and others also.

READING GOOD LITERATURE

There are certain subjects I feel are important enough to be studied on a more regular basis, and have so altered my unit studies. I feel that books of high literary content should be read aloud to the children on a daily basis. These include timeless classics, Newbery Award Books, and books that have merited other awards. I try to read one chapter or a substantial bit of a chapter from such a book each day.

Often, we break from our unit of study and take some time out to concentrate on the particular book I'm reading aloud. Generally, I have the children engaged in a writing activity centered around this book. I may have the older children write two pages about any part of the book. Sometimes, I have them create their own stories that in some way relate to the story we're reading. For instance, after reading **The Indian in the Cupboard** (a book about a plastic Indian that comes to life when placed in an old cupboard, locked with a special key), I asked my girls to write a three-page story about a toy that comes to life. They wrote imaginative stories, each completely different even though they had both been inspired by the same book.

I have separate story times with my two older girls and my two younger boys. They like having a more individualized story time. Even so, I still read books of high literary value to the younger children. They have no trouble with vocabulary above their level or following a complicated story line. If they don't understand something, they ask about it, and

Mason called such works "living books," and her own extensive experience as an educator had demonstrated conclusively that when a child has an ongoing relationship with such books, he or she is willingly participating in the most effective form of education.

With good reason, Charlotte Mason equated the use of "living books" with the spreading of a lavish feast, full of flavor and nourishment, before children.
—Elizabeth Wilson
Books Children Love,
published by Crossway Books

The child who enters school with a background of having been extensively conversed with and read to for all of his or her life, has received the best possible preparation for language skills.
—Diane Lopez
Teaching Children,
published by Crossway Books

we discuss it. They like the fact that I take the time to answer their questions. Even children who have not had more difficult books read aloud to them in the past will in time grow accustomed to having these books read to them and even find them very enjoyable. It may take a little time, but hang in there! My baby also wants to be included in story time. Sometimes she nurses while I read to the other children, or she plays quietly. She has special books I read to her, and she has books she can freely look through. I know not all young children have an attention span for this, but you can build that attention span in them. Even babies should have picture books read to them each day.

My younger children are too young to write down their thoughts about the books I read aloud to them. Sometimes they retell the story or a portion of it to me. Sometimes they copy one or two key sentences that I choose from the book. They often make an illustration to go along with the book.

Most of these kinds of books contain dialogue, making excellent selections for dictation to older children and giving practice using commas, quotation marks, and beginning a new line when a different character speaks. Some writing activities can be as simple as having your children make lists of various things, people, or places in the story. You can have them compare or contrast two characters in the story. If you are still in the midst of reading the book, you can have them write their own ending. If you feel you need more ideas for writing assignments, there are many creative writing books on the market.

One useful book is entitled, *If You're Trying to Teach Kids to Write, You've Gotta Have This Book*. This book emphasizes that not all writing has to be creative writing but can be writing pertaining to every-day life. But for the most part, you can come up with ideas on your own or use ideas from other mothers.

True enough, in less than half an hour they had crossed a dyke of solid masonry, and were in the very heart of the great metropolis of the Netherlands—a walled city of ninety-five islands and nearly two hundred bridges. Although Ben had been there twice since his arrival in Holland, he saw much to excite wonder; but his Dutch comrades, having lived near by all their lives, considered it the most matter-of-course place in the world. Everything interested Ben: the tall houses with their forked chimneys and gable ends facing the street; the merchants' warerooms, perched high up under the roofs of their dwellings, with long, armlike cranes hoisting and lowering goods past the household windows; the grand public buildings erected upon wooden piles driven deep into the marshy ground; the narrow streets; the canals everywhere crossing the city; the bridges; the locks; the various costumes, and strangest of all, shops and dwellings crouching close to the fronts of the churches, sending their long, disproportionate chimneys far upward along the sacred walls.
—Hans Brinker
By Mary Mapes Dodge, published by Grosset and Dunlap, Inc.

To add variety to our lessons, we take a portion of our study time and devote it to taking a closer look at a pleasurable book I am reading aloud to my children. You might say that we are maintaining a continuing literary unit.

Fictional books can be used to enhance your study. For example, a unit involving the study of animals is an easy one for locating fictional books about these animals. While engaged in our world geography unit, we read a fictional story that took place in Japan, and it did much to open our eyes to the customs and beliefs of that country. These kinds of books add a little flavor to your study. Authors of fictional novels generally have extensive knowledge of their subject and location of their story. E. B. White's fictional story, **The Trumpet of the Swan,** although about a swan who could perform human-like tasks, was very real in its depiction of the geographical locations of the swan's travels.

Integrating classics and historical novels into your unit studies is an effective teaching method; however, reverse this technique, allowing the classics or novels to be the main emphasis of your study. Choose a classic relating to a specific time period and/or place you wish to study. Skim through the book noting key people, places, events, discoveries, inventions, trades, and so on. This method is similar to the textbook-unit study method I earlier described in the section **Getting Started.**

A book such as Robert Louis Stevenson's **Treasure Island** lends itself to a study of pirates, the ocean, islands, ships, navigational terms, the author himself, and his other works such as a **A Child's Garden of Verses.** We spent a couple of months on this study, reading **Treasure Island** and making a video of an excerpt from the book. The children and I made all the costumes and scenery, and my oldest

44

daughter filmed the performance. We employed two other home-educated boys as pirates. During this time, my children also wrote their own 16-page books as we studied literary styles. We read *A Child's Garden of Verses,* spurring many creative writing assignments and art projects.

There are many excellent classics relating to early America. The **Little House** books, by Laura Ingalls Wilder, are a marvelous choice for a pioneer literary unit. As I read **By the Shores of Silver Lake** with my two boys, we made a brief study of the early trains in America. Laura, Mary, Carrie, Grace and Ma experienced their first train ride as they crossed the prairie by rail to join Pa in Dakota Territory. A study of the terrain and climate of the Midwest would be advantageous while reading these books. You might also study locusts, malaria, mosquitoes, flowers, grasses, westward expansion, circuit preachers, farming, fiddles, Old West towns, one-room schools, territories and statehood, muskrats, prairie hens, prairie dogs, wolves, log cabins, and the list continues.

Lois Lenski's books such as *Strawberry Girl, Peanuts for Billy Ben, To Be a Logger, Shoo-fly Girl* and several others are excellent in their depiction of the people from specific regions and times in our country's past.

Heidi, Hans Brinker, Swiss Family Robinson and *The Cat Who Went to Heaven* are a few classics whose stories are based in other countries. One friend of mine suggests that *Swiss Family Robinson* be used as a springboard for an interesting and intense science unit. This book describes numerous habitats, animals, plant life and land formations. It depicts a strong love for our Creator; it places a heavy emphasis on character building, industry, creativity and physical development. Not to mention its literary excellence surpasses most books written

The train was coming, louder. They stood by the satchels on the platform and saw it coming. Laura did not know how they could get the satchels on the train. Ma's hands were full, and Laura had to hold onto Mary. The engine's round front window glared in the sunshine like a huge eye. The smokestack flared upward to a wide top, and black smoke rolled up from it. A sudden streak of white shot up through the smoke, then the whistle screamed a long wild scream. The roaring thing came rushing straight at them all, swelling bigger and bigger, enormous, shaking everything with noise.
Then the worst was over. It had not hit them; it was roaring by them on thick big wheels. Bumps and crashes ran along the freight cars and flat cars and they stopped moving. The train was there, and they had to get into it.
—By the Shores of Silver Lake
By Laura Ingalls Wilder, published by Harper and Row

today. Even a simple task or event is described in an eloquent fashion.

While reading classics you will find many and varied details, such as I've briefly mentioned, providing you with plenty of interesting material to study. I strongly encourage you to read the unabridged versions of these timeless books in order to benefit from their rich vocabulary and literary superiority.

The Foundation for American Christian Education publishes materials incorporating the notebook approach, emphasizing the study of **Key Classics on the Chain of Christianity.**

Books Children Love is a prime source for locating appealing classics to serve as a basis for your studies. Use your imagination and develop your own classic units. This will prove a rewarding experience as you share these books with your children. I've found the books are even more enthralling when we read them for a second time.

FINE ARTS

The fine arts is another area I feel is very important to study. All too often we overlook the fine arts in favor of more academic endeavors. Fine arts can be integrated into many units of study, or the study can center entirely around the life of a poet, artist, or composer.

As I mentioned earlier in the section on **Using the Library,** we conducted a study of the American Revolution and learned about the painters of that time. This allowed us to view that time period through the artistic eye. We enjoyed reading about the painters' lives and viewing their works from library books. The subject card catalogue in the fine arts section of your public library enables you to locate art work pertaining to your unit of study.

During a study such as this, it is enjoyable for the children to try their hand at painting.

Poetry is a wonderful avenue to explore when engaged in almost any unit. You can locate poems about boats, trains, seasons, astronomy, the ocean, animals, and so forth. (The Library Reference Guide located at the end of this book will aid you in your search for poems pertaining to your unit.)

A simple way to locate poems relating to your study is to select a large volume of poetry with a subject index. Look up words pertinent to your study. If you have difficulty locating volumes with a subject index, browse through the title index, for many first words of titles are indicative of their subject matter. This is also true of first lines of poems, and many poetry volumes also have indexes of first lines.

Music of a particular time period or geographical location can be integrated into your unit study. We plan to study the music of the Revolution. There are several songbooks relating to the Revolutionary period that include the music, words, and historical background of each song. Our library contains a videotape, *The Music of Williamsburg.*

Hear and Learn Publications offers tapes and songbooks, tracing United States history through song. The titles now available are *History Alive Through Music—America,* and *History Alive Through Music—Westward Ho!*

While studying a particular country, you can examine the accomplishments of one of its composers of the past or present. There are many interesting children's biographies telling of the great composers' lives. Check out audio cassette tapes featuring works of a chosen composer, and have your children write a poem to accompany a particular musical selection. They might enjoy

The list of Christians involved in the arts and human expression through history is almost endless and would form many volumes in itself. The names Bach, van Eyck, Vermeer, the names of Handel, Mendelssohn, Haydn, writers such as Shakespeare, the artists of the early Italian Renaissance, many many hundreds, perhaps even thousands of names could be searched out as those who were either personally Bible-believing Christians themselves, with real and living faith, or at the very least those who operated unquestioningly within the Christian consensus, taking strength and shelter from its framework.
—Franky Schaeffer
Addicted to Mediocrity, published by Crossway Books

Praise the Lord! Praise God in His sanctuary; Praise Him in His mighty expanse. Praise Him for His mighty deeds; Praise Him according to His excellent greatness. Praise Him with trumpet sound; Praise Him with harp and lyre. Praise Him with timbrel and dancing; Praise Him with stringed instrument and pipe. Praise Him with loud cymbals. Let everything that has breath praise the Lord. Praise the Lord!
Psalm 150
(NASV)

writing a song and even composing the music.

Fine art, music and poetry add a more enjoyable and refreshing air to our studies. This type of study also serves to activate the children's creativities.

Several published curriculums are available to enhance your fine art studies. The Cornerstone Curriculum Project offers **Music and Moments with the Masters** and **Adventures in Art.** The Classic Plan offers a program integrating fine art, poetry, and music into a common theme. Fine art prints of various sizes can be ordered from the National Gallery of Art in Washington, D.C.

NATURE STUDIES

In Charlotte Mason's book entitled **Home Education,** she strongly emphasizes the need for children to become thoroughly acquainted with nature. She states:

> ...she will point to some lovely flower or gracious tree, not only as a beautiful work, but a beautiful thought of God, in which we may believe He finds continual pleasure, and which He is pleased to see his human children rejoice in. [14]

Miss Mason advocates taking nature walks, collecting berries, sticks, wild flowers, leaves, and so forth. She makes an entire lesson of this in which the children then make drawings of the items collected. She also suggests identifying these specimens. (This can be done using paperback field guides. The guides are quite inexpensive and fairly easy to use.)

The first time we decided to undertake a nature mini-unit, my children and I went on a short walk down the alley behind our house and were amazed at how many interesting plants, mushrooms, leaves, and wild flowers we could find. We took our treasures home and drew the specimens we liked best. We also located these specimens in the field guides. Two hours later I informed my children that we had done enough for one day, but they all wanted to continue making more sketches. I had them date their drawings and put them in a folder designated for their nature mini-unit. I decided to incorporate this nature mini-unit into our course of study, whereby on the third Monday of each month this study is our main thrust.

We recently studied the Dutch artist Jan van Huysum. My son Raymond noticed right away how van Huysum had painted insects on his flowers, and this really fascinated Raymond. Now these insects were extremely small, and I hardly noticed them myself, but Raymond was very observant. As we were sketching the leaves and so forth that we had gathered on our walk, Raymond said he wanted to draw a bug on his leaf. Well, at just that moment a bug walked onto his paper and posed for him; Raymond was very excited. Afterwards, we pressed the leaves and flowers.

USING THE BIBLE

I'd like to spend a few minutes discussing the integration of the Bible into your unit studies. Another factor common to several published unit study curriculums is the integration of Scripture into the study. By using a concordance, I'm able to find Scriptures that relate to my particular unit of study. For instance, when we were working on our world geography unit, I looked up words in my concordance like mountain, valley, sea, earth, and river. We studied the creation account in Genesis chapter one, and the older girls used this Scripture for typing practice.

(I checked out a children's typing manual from the library and spent about two months on intense typing instruction. Now my girls maintain their typing skills by typing biblical excerpts pertaining to

"The difficult march was at length over, and we emerged from the forest upon a large plain covered with curious little bushes. The branches of these little shrubs and the ground about them were covered with pure-white flakes."

"Snow! Snow!" exclaimed Franz. "Oh, mother, come down from the cart and play snowballs. This is jolly; much better than ugly rain."

"I was not surprised by the boy's mistake, for indeed the flakes did look like snow. But before I could express my opinion, Fritz declared that the plant must be a kind of dwarf cotton tree. We approached nearer and found he was right—soft fine wool enclosed in pods, and still hanging on the bushes or lying on the ground, abounded in every direction. We had indeed discovered this valuable plant."
—Swiss Family Robinson
By Johann Wyss, published by Grosset and Dunlap, Inc.

Five principles for educating our children are revealed clearly in the fountainhead of all biblical texts on education, Deuteronomy 6:4-9.

In this passage we find the purpose of education, the primary site of instruction, the specific curriculum, the designated faculty, and the most effective methods of instruction. By looking at these principles, we can see the biblical basis for home education.
—Gregg Harris
"The Biblical Basis for Home Education," The Teaching Home, *Aug./Sept. 1990*

our particular unit of study. Some of these passages are used for memorizing. A large print Bible works well for the children's typing exercises. We have a word processor, but even an electric typewriter would be a good investment. It is advantageous for your children to learn the typing basics. For some families, a personal computer is a valuable instrument. Computers will change many times over before our children are ready to obtain a job, but keyboard experience will have lasting benefits.)

Generally, a concordance will point you to key passages that deal with your unit, but this is not exhaustive. For example, when studying astronomy, a concordance can be used to look up related terms such as *star, constellation, sun, moon,* and *heavens,* since these specific words appear in biblical passages. A topical Bible will point you to many passages that would be missed by only utilizing a concordance. When using a topical Bible, such as **Nave's Topical Bible**, you can directly look up *astronomy* and it will lead you to related passages without requiring you to have prior knowledge of the subject matter.

If you are studying a particular painter, for instance, it may prove difficult to use a concordance to locate biblical material relating to your study. If you are reading the biography of this individual, you could ask yourself what character qualities this man or woman possessed. You would then be able to proceed to a topical Bible and look up these specific qualities. This could be true of negative qualities as well, such as drunkenness or pride. You could investigate what the Bible has to say about such things. This helps your children to learn to discern character traits in others and evaluate their own growth.

Don't feel as if you have to try to spiritualize everything. Those things which are sinful are to be avoided, but all other things are a very real part of our Christian lives. Our Heavenly Father created the whole universe; therefore, any and all of His creation is worthy to be studied. In his book, *Addicted to Mediocrity,* Franky Schaeffer states:

> Things do not need spiritual or theological justification. They are what they are—as God made them. We are those who have been freed to truly see the world as it is and enjoy and revel in the diversity and beauty that God has made. Not everything needs to be justified in terms of tacking on a few Christian slogans at the end to somehow redeem it. Christ redeems what we do. We do not need to redeem it with slogans. There is no Christian world, no secular world, these are just words. There is only one world— the world God made![5]

It is crucial that our children see how Scripture relates to all of life. Everything for an abundant life can be learned from these pages. Too often Christian curriculums do a tacky job of integrating Scripture into a lesson. We can show our children how Scripture is the basis for all of life. We can also teach our children how to use biblical study aids to find desired information. A concordance is fairly easy to use.

In our study on the human body, my children typed and memorized Psalm 139:13–16, the account of the infant in its mother's womb. They also used various other passages as typing assignments. We looked up words in the concordance such as *eye, body* and *blood.* After reviewing several of the verses listed, I picked some appropriate for typing, dictation or memorization assignments.

I am much afraid that the schools will prove the very gates of hell, unless they diligently labor in explaining the Holy Scriptures, and engraving them in the hearts of youth. I advise no one to place his child where the Scriptures do not reign paramount. Every institution in which men are not unceasingly occupied with the Word of God must be corrupt.
—Martin Luther

51

RECORD-KEEPING

I use a daily log. I find it is convenient to enter the material covered daily as we go along. Planning ahead has its merits, but I find lesson plans cannot always be strictly followed. Too many things come up as we proceed through our study. It is advantageous to have your basic outline for the material you intend to cover; then enter the actual material covered in your log. If you have your log filled out neatly ahead of time, you will be less likely to deviate from it and thus lose those teachable moments. When your children ask a question pertaining to your study, you should have the flexibility to use that opportunity to teach something perhaps not on that day's lesson plan. If they ask something that you can't answer yourself, then you have the flexibility to research that topic together. There are also times when you cannot cover all the material you have planned. Perhaps it will take longer than you anticipated. It's very frustrating if you have all your plans neatly logged and then you can't accomplish them all. At times you may feel the need to force your children to finish what you've written down previously, to avoid disrupting your log. Let your lesson plans work for you as a general guide, not against you like a task master.

I use a spiral notebook to record our progress because it is easy to write in, inexpensive compared to lesson planning books, easy to store, can be left open to the current page, and is flexible, not filled with graphs and charts that don't suit my purpose.

I print the beginning date on the cover of my daily log book with a permanent marker. When the book is filled, I put the ending date on the cover as well and keep these log books for future reference. I designate one page for each day of the week;

I combine Saturday and Sunday on one page to be used for logging books read or listened to and any other educational endeavors. In the top right-hand corner I write the date and day of the week. Even on days we don't do schoolwork, I date the page and enter anything pertinent such as field trips, games played, books read, projects accomplished, physical activities, and so forth.

I use one book for record-keeping for my four children. I use two pages daily, writing the information for each child on one side of each page. You may wish to have a logbook for each of your children, as this may eliminate confusion in record-keeping for the purpose of presenting information to local officials if necessary.

I use a number of abbreviations for logging material, and as you proceed you will devise your own system. I write the full title and author of any books we use. This makes a handy reference guide for future studies. It prevents occurrences such as, Now what was the name of that book we used when we studied geography? I remember it was such a good book. Do not think that you'll be able to recall all this information. Write it down. Be sure to log your studies on a daily basis. Don't assume you can just go back and fill in the days. After a while, one day seems to flow into another.

Keep your log simple. Be sure to include extra-curricular activities. Physical Education can be logged as anything from biking to basketball. I list cooking, sewing, or cleaning under Home Ec. If the child has done a special picture or project, I log it under Art or Projects. Remember, education does not end with school work. Many valuable lessons are learned throughout the day. Older children can also be taught to keep a log of their studies. This would be an excellent lesson in itself. I'm personally going to try this with my two older girls once I've filled up

In the evening, when our room was illuminated with wax candles, I wrote a journal of all the events, which had occurred since our arrival in this foreign land. And, while the mother was busy with her needle and Ernest was making sketches of birds, beasts, and flowers with which he had met during the past months, Fritz and Jack taught little Franz to read.
—Swiss Family Robinson,
By Johann Wyss, published by Grosset and Dunlap, Inc.

our current log book.

Sample Day From Log:

Date/Day

MICHELLE:
Bible: Dad read aloud from *Once a Carpenter*, by Bill Counts
Math: *Saxon 65*—test 16
Listning Comp: Mom read chapter 5 from *Mrs. Frisby and the Rats of NIHM*, by O'Brien
Silent Rdng: *Hatchet*, by Gary Paulsen
Home Ec: sewing—made doll clothes
P.E.: roller skating
Human Body Unit:
Dictation: "The Supportive System" from the book *Your Body and How it Works*, by Wong
Oral Rdng and Listning Comp: *The Skeleton Inside You*, by Philip Balestrino. (Michelle, Melissa and Mom took turns reading aloud and read entire book)
Experiment: "Can You Change Your Height Overnight?"—from *Your Bo ly and How it Works*, by Wong
Typing: Psalm 139:13-16

Date/Day

MELISSA:
Bible: Dad read from *Once a Carpenter*, by Counts
Math: *Addison-Wesley*, 4th grade, pp 27, 28
Listning Comp: Mom read aloud ch 5 from *Mrs. Frisby...*
Home Ec: baked cookies
P.E.: roller skating
Silent Rdng: two chapters from *Little House in the Big Woods*, by Laura Ingalls Wilder.
Human Body Unit:
Dictation: "The Supportive System"/*Your Body and How it Works*
Oral Rdng and Listning Comp: *The Skeleton Inside You*, by Balestrino
Experiment: "Can You Change Your Height Overnight?"/*Yr Bdy and Hw it Wks*
Typing: Psalm 139:13-16

Date/Day

ROBERT:
Bible: Dad read aloud from *Once a Carpenter*
Piano Lessons
Phonics: "le" as in "bottle," "little," etc., also explained about double const. Robt wrote and spelled words himself, also reviewed "baby," "happy," etc.
Listning Comp: Mom read aloud from *The Trumpet of the Swan*, by E.B. White, chapter 2
Math: 100 Board Activity
Art Proj: painted a T-shirt
P.E.: roller skating

Human Body Unit:
Listning Comp: Mom read entire book, *The Skeleton Inside You*, by Balestrino
Copy Work: From above book, "Bones give you shape. Bones are hard."
Oral Rdng: Robt read these sentences aloud

Date/Day

RAYMOND:
Bible: Dad read from *Once a Carpenter*
Phonics Work: "ay," "sh," silent "e" in long vowel words
Listning Comp: Mom read ch 2 from *The Trumpet of the Swan*
Math: 100 Board Activity
Art Proj: painted a T-shirt
P.E.: roller skating
Human Body Unit:
Listning Comp: Mom read *The Skeleton Inside You*, by Balestrino
Copy Work: "Bones give you shape."
Oral Rdng: Raymond read sentence aloud

Generally, I use abbreviations more extensively. For sake of clarity, I did not in my sample log. As you can see from the sample log, a good portion of our school day is composed of reading. A lot of busy work is eliminated, thereby giving us valuable time for reading.

As I stated earlier, we conduct math studies in addition to our unit studies to get plenty of practice with the basic skills. We integrate the math into our studies whenever possible. Math skills are also integrated into our daily lives. I also mentioned that I read aloud each day from a book noted for its literary value. This too is separate from our unit study and is listed under Listening Comprehension. They're listening to me read and they're comprehending what's being read, at least to some degree. How do I know they're comprehending? Because they want me to go on. They're excited about what we are reading. Generally, people aren't too interested in material they can't understand. It is also beneficial to discuss what you have read and occasionally have each child narrate all or a portion of what you have read. This narration was one of Charlotte Mason's favorite exercises for children. I usually read this good literature at bedtime. It is a pleasant way to end the day.

You will notice a section on my sample daily log marked Oral Reading and Listening Comprehension. This oral reading pertains to our unit study and is shared by my two girls and me. They benefit from reading aloud and listening to others. This reading is usually from a biography corresponding to our unit study. This is not always the case (as you can see in the sample daily log, we were reading a book about the skeleton).

My children do not type every day, nor do they write from dictation every day. They generally perform some writing activity on a daily basis though. I try to use a number of approaches to teach each unit so that the children receive the benefits of a variety of techniques. Hopefully, this section pertaining to the daily log will give you a basic format to create a system of recording that works best for you. You may choose to be more or less formal in your record-keeping as you find what suits your needs.

As we consider logging the academic accomplishments of our children, we should also consider their other endeavors. Do you realize the importance of training your children not only in academics but in life skills? As home educators, we are often unjustly accused of sheltering our children from the real world, when in actuality we possess the greater potential for sharing the real world with our children. Is the real world six or seven hours a day with your peers studying isolated subjects that are seldom integrated and even less frequently related to the real world? I think not. (If the real world is obscenity, sexual perversion, disrespect for authority, and so on, then by all means I want to shelter my child from that! I want to shelter myself as well.)

We must ask ourselves, for what purpose are we training our children? Are we training them to become academic robots or self-sufficient individuals with abilities in many areas?

Our society has become so specialized that people concentrate solely on a specific field and are nearly ignorant in every other field. We are taught to leave most things to the professionals, and in doing so we have lost our abilities to do for ourselves.

What I'm trying to say is that there is more to education than academics. Don't our children need to learn how to cook, clean, sew, grocery shop, care for others, plan a household budget, pay bills, work on the car, make home repairs, garden, mow the lawn, teach, and so on? Or should they leave matters to the professionals?

I think because society has distorted the true meaning of education, we often overlook these crucial areas in favor of concentrating on more academic endeavors. I used to feel guilty if I took time from academics to teach my children some of these skills. I thought I was depriving them of a good education, but in reality a well-rounded education encompasses real-life skills. I was apprehensive about training them in these less-academic areas because I had nothing tangible, such as a written piece of work, to show that I was indeed instructing my child. If my child spent forty-five minutes on a math page, I then had proof that education was truly taking place. But if my child spent two hours planning and preparing a meal, there was nothing tangible to represent this as education, although many skills are necessary to perform this task.

I realize that if I somehow document this educational experience, I will have the proof or record I desire to show that education is indeed taking place. Well, then comes the problem of documenting this kind of learning experience. I devise names for these various learning experiences or life-training skills or other activities my children are involved in. Cooking can be listed under Culinary Arts or Home Economics, including a list of the dishes prepared. Gardening can be listed under Agricultural Studies, housework listed under Domestic Engineering, changing the oil in the car recorded under Auto Maintenance, and babysitting logged under Child Care or Child Development.

Have your older child plan the family meals for a week. You can record this as Dietary Planning. Do your children like to draw, make art projects, paper crafts, and so on? Log these as Creative Expression or Art. Do your children clip coupons and help you grocery shop? This is Food Budget Analysis and Planning. Do your children set up a store or library and play for hours at this? This can be logged as Role Play. Do your children fold laundry, sweep floors, clean tables, dust, make beds, vacuum, clean bathrooms, practice an instrument, play ball, ride bikes, skate, invent games, play board games, play card games, collect stamps, cross-stitch, knit, whittle, sing, sew, paint, wash the car or attend outside activities? If the answer is *yes* to any of these, then you can devise a category to log these educational experiences. What kinds of things do your children do all day? If they sit around and watch TV or play video games, then your logbook may be nearly blank, but if they're involved in real-life activities, even on a day when schoolwork isn't implemented, you should be able to just about fill a page with the educational activities of each of your children.

Do you read the Bible daily? Record the passages read under Bible Studies. Do your children read on their own? Record the title and author under Silent Reading. Do you read aloud to your children each day? Record the title, author, and chapters read under Listening Comprehension. Do your children read aloud to you or their siblings? Record the title, author, and chapters read under Oral Reading. These are daily occurrences in our home, along with chores.

Biking, swimming, skating, playing at a park, or making and using an obstacle course can be logged as Physical Education. If you meet regularly with other home-educating families at a park or central location for play and fellowship, this can be recorded as Physical Education and Socialization Skills.

Do you ever attend plays, visit the zoo, investigate museums, and explore nature? Log these activities as Field Trips. It isn't necessary that these activities be done with a group to qualify as a field trip. We prefer to do these things as a family whenever possible because the children don't seem as distracted.

As you begin to keep a daily log of all of the different things your children do along with their more academic endeavors, you will begin to see what makes up a real, well-balanced curriculum. A friend of mine began using this method of log-keeping. One day one of her sons saw her entering information about what he had done that day for school and he exclaimed, "I did all that!" Even he was impressed when he was able to see it recorded on paper. Children can also be taught to keep a log of their activities. This is a great way of teaching them to organize their thoughts as well as providing them with practice in language arts skills.

A long time ago, the Dutch sailors used to figure how fast they were going by throwing a piece of wood—they called it a log—overboard. One man stood forward in the bow of the ship and threw the log into the water. Another man stood aft, in the stern of the ship, and kept track of how many seconds it took until the stern of the ship passed the log. They knew how many seconds it took for the ship to go that many feet, they could figure out how many knots it was making. That was the way they measured their speed. They said they logged their speed because they figured it with a log. And that's why we call this pie-shaped piece of wood a log; because we use it to log the speed of the ship—you see?"

Nat squared his shoulders. "So now I know what it means to keep a log."

Sam bellowed, "No! That isn't keeping a log! Keeping a log is keeping the record of what happens on the voyage."

Nat said, "Then why don't they call it keeping a record?"

"Because one of the most important things in the record is the speed they have logged; so they call the whole record of what happens the log."
—Carry On Mr. Bowditch, *By Jean Lee Latham, published by Houghton Mifflin Company*

We must realize that all learning is not adult contrived. Children will learn on their own, as it is their nature to explore. We should expose them to a variety of things, provide them with materials to be creative, and be available to help and answer questions. We also need to know when to leave well enough alone and allow them to explore and experience failure and success on their own.

It is difficult to achieve a well-rounded education when we're in bondage to textbooks or workbooks, because we feel this ever-present pressure to complete the book. This leaves little time for other endeavors such as learning how to hang wallpaper, make cookies, wash clothes, paint the house, plan a meal, plant a garden, and so on. Or, perhaps you are Supermom and can juggle the textbooks, piano lessons, little league, soccer practice and real-life skills. I've tried playing that game before, and I'm glad to say I gave it up for something better. I gave it up for peace of mind and a happy household.

If you are using workbooks, textbooks or a curriculum, feel free to break away and spend some time teaching your children how to cook, garden or sew. What would be the loss of finishing a text in twelve months instead of nine, if you were able to have a host of other real-life experiences. If this would cause a problem, then you should re-evaluate your educational program, because anything that would place such restrictions on your family can only be detrimental to their education. If it's the system or a book that's imprisoning you, isn't it time you are set free?

Perhaps keeping a log of all your children's activities will help you realize how much learning is really taking place each day. I know it has helped to set me free, so as to enable my children to get on with real life.

REFLECTING ON UNIT STUDIES

For several years now, my family has been using the unit study approach to learning. My children's attitudes about schoolwork have changed. They are interested in our studies and eager to learn. We occasionally have problems but not nearly so often as when we used textbooks and workbooks.

My attitude has changed because I too am eager to learn. I see my attitude reflected in their eyes. We must set a good example for our children to follow. They also know that much of the material we are learning is new to me also. We're learning together. They quiz me on material that we are trying to memorize. They see that it is a challenge for me, too. I have to look up words in the dictionary just as they do. I discuss my strong points and my weak points with them openly. They know I'm a real person. They know I'm still learning and growing. They know learning lasts a lifetime.

They aren't bound by graded textbooks or by learning labels. They are free to learn at a rate that is appropriate for them. They are free of busy work and boring work. My children know that if they're interested in a particular topic that we will supply them with the necessary elements so they can pursue their interests. They are free to be different from anyone else and still feel loved and accepted and valuable. They are individuals with their own needs, talents, and desires. If you can tap into your children's interests and help them cultivate those interests, they will begin to learn and explore on their own.

As we've progressed through our unit studies and read numerous biographies of people from all walks of life, one common thread we have noticed amongst them is that they were not ordinary. Their education

Character education is the missing link. The highest goal of teaching at its best is character education. It is bringing to our children/students lessons of love which breed concern for others—putting them ahead of ourselves. It is showing by example that honesty, dependability, neatness, order, industry, and initiative richly pay. It is teaching the equality of human beings by practicing the Golden Rule. It is demonstrating to children how to work and how to help, instead of waiting for things to be done for them. It is teaching them to feel needed and wanted and depended upon—in order to develop a sense of self-worth. The child who has this advantage generally becomes a self-directed leader in his society. He knows where he is going and is not easily pressured by his peers.
—Raymond and Dorothy Moore
Home Style Teaching, *published by Word Books Publisher*

was very different from what we know today. They pursued their interests with zealousness. For example, when conducting our studies on children's authors, we read a biography about Beatrix Potter, author of **The Tale of Peter Rabbit.** She was schooled at home by a governess. They took numerous nature walks and collected flowers, fungi, and small animals. From these specimens, Beatrix would make sketches and study them in great detail, learning all she could about them. Her governess noticed her interest and talent and encouraged her in further pursuit of this interest. Beatrix Potter spent a couple of hours each day at a wildlife museum. She wasn't bored to tears with textbooks. She was gently guided in the things she had an affinity toward. Her grandmother encouraged her to be bold and different. And, therefore, a great author and illustrator of children's books was nurtured to fruition.

While reading biographies of famous people, point out the ways in which these people were different from those around them and from those today. Realizing, of course, that you will not want to emulate all those you read about. However, certain traits they bore may be worthy of emulation. Help your children to appreciate that they too are different. This is important for their self-esteem, especially when schools today try to press the masses into the same mold. It seems that this pressure causes children to regret being different from others. Different is considered good only if your child is in the gifted program. But all children are special and deserve a specially tailored curriculum. Think just how special each child is to our Heavenly Father.

As we study art, music, math, science, history and literature, we get a glimpse of the different lifestyles and personalities of real individuals. We begin to appreciate the beauty in these things and in the world around us. Open up new and previously unexplored areas for your children. You never know what might spark their interests.

Sandi Patti sings a song about the creation of the world that goes like this: "He could have made it black and white and we'd have never known."[16] Let's help our children to lead a life full of color. It's very difficult to encourage the development of extraordinary individuals with an ordinary curriculum. Let's not re-establish the ordinary classroom in our homes. We have a much greater potential than this, for we were created in His image. Through this realization of the importance of each individual as fashioned in His image, we can influence our children in understanding the importance of service toward others; family first, and then those less fortunate than ourselves. We want to raise self-sacrificing individuals, not self-seeking persons.

Begin with a unit you can easily manage and progress to a more detailed topic. Don't exhaust yourself by taking on too much at first. Don't be intimidated by others who appear to have it all together. Use any helpful advice they may have to offer and don't worry about the rest. We are all constantly learning; for remember, learning lasts a lifetime. It's important that you hang in there and don't give up. You will reap the rewards of perseverance.

We read in James 1:5, "But if any of you lacks wisdom, let him ask God, who gives to all men generously and without reproach, and it will be given to him." (NASV)[17]

"I want to see my sons strong, both morally and physically," said I. "That means, little Franz," as the large blue eyes looked inquiringly up at me, "brave to do what is good and right, and to hate evil, and strong to work, hunt, and provide for themselves and others, and to fight if necessary."
—Swiss Family Robinson
By Johann Wyss, published by Grosset and Dunlap, Inc.

SAMPLE UNITS

On the next several pages, you will find some sample units. (Also included are two sample units conducted by others.) They are not intended to be used in a step-by-step fashion but are rather to be viewed as something that we did as a family. I would never expect anyone to try to follow my plan, just as it would be extremely difficult for me to follow someone else's plan. The key to a successful unit study is for you to pick an interesting topic, raid your library for books, tapes, and other materials, and see how you can fit these into your schedule. Perhaps you will only pick a few books for younger children, a few books for older children and one or two books to be read aloud. We happen to have a family that devours books, as it is evident from our sample units that follow. Remember, you can fit in a lot more good books when you eliminate the busy work. It is important to keep things as simple as possible, especially in the beginning.

Note: Some of the books listed were read aloud together, with the older children taking turns reading along with Mom. Some of the books were read silently by some of the children. Some of the books were read entirely aloud by Mom or Dad. And finally, some of the books were read aloud entirely by the children. This was all done according to needs and abilities. It is not necessary to read this many books to satisfactorily complete a unit. Even though it seems we read a lot of books, we really just brush the surface when it comes to the vast wealth of books written for children. Remember, in any unit you pursue you cannot possibly cover all the material available on that subject. Use the materials that work best for your family. Don't try to take on too much at first; you can always go back and cover a unit more thoroughly at a future date. Relax and enjoy your family.

Sample Unit:

WORLD GEOGRAPHY UNIT

Activities and Creative Writing Assignments: Went on vacation and collected postcards, brochures, etc.; the children made a scrapbook and entered in information about each place visited. Worked on map-reading skills while on our trip. "Create a Country"—made a card with important information on it about an imaginary country, made accompanying flag and a map, gave brief description of the people. Filled in names of countries on map for each continent. Made a list of geography terms to use for writing a poem, and then wrote poems. Wrote a story about a mouse on Columbus' ship. Drew North and South poles, equator, and lines of latitude on an orange. Wrote a story using geographical terms and made a map to go with the story. For each biography read, we made time-line figures. Collected stamps, which included stamps from countries all over the world. Measured distances on a map using a scale. Made a list of geography terms from A to Z. Made a list of countries from A to Z. Located points on the map of the world using degrees of longitude and latitude. Made maps of interior of house. Made maps of neighborhood.

Games and Puzzles: *Where in the World?*, *Map of the World Puzzle* jigsaw puzzle, and *Map of the World Puzzle* wooden Judy Puzzle.

Non-Fiction Books Read: *The Columbus Story,* by Alice Dalgliesh. *Balboa, Finder of the Pacific,* by Ronald Syme. *Francisco Pizzaro, Finder of Peru,* by Ronald Syme. *Magellan, First Around the World,* by Syme. *A World Explorer, Ponce De Leon,* by Wyatt Blassingame. *John Cabot and His Son Sebastian,* by Syme. *Vasco Da Gama,* by Syme. *Pop-up Atlas of* *the World,* by Theodore Rowland Entwistle. *Looking at Maps,* by Erich Fuchs. *Maps and Globes,* by Knowlton. *Marco Polo,* by Ceserani. *Nigerian Pioneer,* by Syme. *New World History and Geography,* published by A Beka (used to dictate from or read about selected countries in each region or continent studied). *African Journey,* by John Chiasson, and *Explorers in Africa,* by Richard Seymour Hall. (These books were used for their pictures.) *The Voyages of Captain Cook,* by Roger Hart. *Where in the World do You Live?,* by Al Hine and John Alcorn. *The Discoverers,* by Grant Neil. (Used portions of this book; good illustrations.) *Shaka, King of the Zulus,* by Diane Stanley.

Fiction Books Read: *Henry the Explorer, Henry Explores the Jungle, Henry and the Castaways,* and *Henry Explores the Mountains,* all by Mark Taylor. (These books were used as an introduction to exploring with my younger children.) *The Happy Orpheline,* and entire Orpheline series, by Natalie Savage Carlson. (This series of stories takes place in France.) *The Cat Who Went to Heaven,* by Elizabeth Coatsworth. (This story takes place in Japan and gives insight into Hinduism.) *Ananda in Sri Lanka,* by Carol Barker.

Terms and Their Definitions Used for Dictation (Source of information, *Nat'l Geographic, Exploring Your World)*: isthmus, country, ocean, the ocean floor, coral reef, peninsula, latitude, longitude, equator, maps and globes, navigation, desert, valley, mountain, volcano, sea, island, tides.

Videos: *India, Morocco, Egypt.*

Audio Cassettes: *Geography Songs* and *More Geography Songs.*

Bible Verses: The following passages were dictated over a period of time. *Genesis* chapter one. *Job* chapter 38. *Isaiah* 40:3-8.

Other Publications: "God's World Newspapers," "The Tampa Tribune."

Field Trips: Museum of Science and Industry, viewed traveling *Spanish Explorer Exhibit.*

Memorization Work: Learned names and locations of all the countries, oceans, and major seas in the world. Memorized portions of *Genesis* Chapter 1.

Sample Unit:

CHILDREN'S AUTHORS UNIT

Activities and Creative Writing Assignments: Viewed and discussed a wide variety of children's books, noting writing styles and illustrations. Wrote three stories, beginning with rough draft, then editing, and then final product. (These books were of varying types: wheel books, flap books, pop-up books, etc.) Some of the stories were typed once they were completely edited; some stories were originally typed on the computer and then edited. The younger children dictated their stories to Mom; the older children helped with typing them. The children made covers for their books and illustrations to go along with their stories. Painted a book jacket and then proceeded to write a story to go with it; the younger children dictated the story to Mom. Younger children drew pictures to accompany various books that Mom read to them. The older children wrote about various accounts they enjoyed most in stories selected by Mom. The older children gave an oral narration to the family of a book they had read. The children participated in reading aloud each day from some of the books listed below. Some creative writing assignments included having the children write a story of their own that patterned one we read together. I gave the children story starters and had them complete the story. The children rewrote a story we had read aloud and changed the ending. The children each wrote and illustrated a book which we "published" ourselves. These books were made like professional books and required five weeks to complete. The book I utilized which gave step-by-step instructions as to how to do this is entitled, *Written and Illustrated by...*, by David Melton. This is an excellent book, and we plan for each child to make another book of this type each year. These are books they will treasure forever.

Games: *Authors Card Game, Children's Authors Card Game.*

Non-Fiction Books Read: *Nothing is Impossible, the Story of Beatrix Potter,* by Dorothy Aldis. *Who Said There's No Man in the Moon? A Story of Jules Verne,* by Robert Quackenbush. *Laura Ingalls Wilder: Growing up in the Little House,* by Patricia Reilly Griff. *Laura Ingalls Wilder,* by Gwenda Blair. *Mark Twain, What Kind of a Name is That?,* by Robert Quackenbush. *The Last Four Years,* by Laura Ingalls Wilder. *To the Point, A Story of E.B. White,* by David R. Collins. *Invincible Louisa,* by Cornelia Meigs. *A Country Artist, A Story About Beatrix Potter,* by David R. Collins. *Little House in the Big Woods,* and others in this series, by Laura Ingalls Wilder.

Fiction Books Read: *The Five Little Peppers and How They Grew,* by Margaret Sidney. *Shoo-fly Girl,* by Lois Lenski. *Peanuts for Billy Ben,* by Lois Lenski. *Christmas Stories,* by Lois Lenski. *Black Star, Bright Dawn,* by Scott O'Dell. *To be a Logger,* by Lois Lenski. *There's Nothing to Do and We Hate Rain,* by James Stevens. *Bayou Suzette,* by Lois Lenski. *The Merry Adventures of Robin Hood,* by Howard Pyle. *The Biggest Bear,* by Lynd Ward. *Little Sioux Girl,* by Lois Lenski. *Eight Cousins,* by Louisa May Alcott. *Hop on Pop,* by Dr. Suess. *Heaven to Betsy,* by Maud Hart Lovelace. *Little Women* and *Jo's Boys,* by Louisa May Alcott. *Strawberry Girl,* by Lenski. *Betsy, Tacey and Tib,* and others in this series, by Lovelace. *Hatchet,* by Gary Paulsen. *The Berenstain Bears and the Week at Grandmas,* and others in this series, by Stan and Jan Berenstain. *Curious Missy,* by Virginia Sorensen. *Miracle on Maple Hill,* by Sorensen. *The Case of the Missing Kittens,* by Mark Taylor. *Stream* to the River, River to the Sea, by Scott O'Dell. *Ida Early Comes Over the Mountain,* by Robert Burch. *The Tale of Peter Rabbit,* and other tales, by Beatrix Potter. *The Plant Sitter,* by Gene Zion. *A Harold Adventure,* by Crockett Johnson, and others in the series. *Bridge to Terabithia,* by Katherine Paterson. *The Indian in the Cupboard, The Return of the Indian,* and *The Secret of the Indian,* by Lynne R. Banks. *Esther Wheelright, Indian Captive,* by Marguerite Vance. *The Box Car Children,* and others in this series, by Gertrude Chandler Warner. *Hattie the Backstage Bat,* and *Corduroy,* by Don Freeman. *Stuart Little, Charlotte's Web,* and *The Trumpet of the Swan,* by E.B. White.

Dictation: Various selections from some of the books we read, especially portions that included dialogue, were utilized for dictation purposes. The younger children did copy work from some of the stories read. I used several of the book jacket, front flap summaries from biographies we read as dictation exercises.

Videos: *Little Women, A Connecticut Yankee in King Arthur's Court, Robin Hood and His Merry Men, The Rats of NIMH, Tom Thumb, Charlotte's Web, 20,000 Leagues Under the Sea* and *Huckleberry Finn.*

Audio Cassettes: *Grimm's Fairy Tales, Robin Hood, Peter Pan,* and cassettes of other various children's stories.

Bible: Discussed and memorized the Ten Commandments with Dad. Read Peter Spier's books, *Noah's Ark* and *Jonah and the Big Fish,* and compared them to the biblical accounts.

Sample Unit:

STORYTELLING UNIT

This unit's primary focus is on oral presentation; therefore, more time is dedicated to the spoken word rather than the written word. It is important that our children learn to express themselves both through the written and the spoken word. Generally, because our society places such a high value on the written word, little emphasis is placed on the spoken word. Also, in a conventional school setting, time doesn't allow for sufficient oral expression experiences. It is for these reasons that I have chosen to conduct this unit. Much time is spent in oral exercises, which are documented in my daily log. Here again, we often feel that learning is not taking place if we don't have a concrete piece of evidence, such as a written piece of work, to document this learning. That is why I document these oral exercises in my daily log.

Initially, I was encouraged to begin this unit because our county was about to have its annual Storytelling Festival. I wanted my children to participate, but I felt it would be too much to take on while in the course of studying another unit. So, I decided we would conduct a storytelling unit to help prepare for the festival. This would give us ample time to prepare and thus reduce the stress of too much work. It is so nice to be able to plan our units around events in the community and family interests without feeling bound to textbooks.

Activities: I obtained the rules and regulations for the festival so as to select suitable materials. No props of any kind were to be used to tell the stories; they were to be strictly narratives. The children and I visited our public library and chose many books, about 75, that we thought might be appropriate for storytelling. The children spent several days reading the books that interested them; the older children and I also read many of these books aloud to the younger children. After becoming familiar with the stories, I helped the children each select an appropriate story to tell. I tried to explain why some books were suitable, and some were not. I explained that books that rely too much on illustrations to convey the story were not good choices for storytelling. I encouraged them to find a book that they could somehow relate to, as this would aid them in their retention of the story. The stories were not to be memorized, except for key phrases and the beginning and ending sentences. Stories should not be acted out, and seldom should you try to use your voice to convey characterization, but rather let the language tell the story.

These tips and other helpful information were obtained from library books. I checked out two books, **Handbook for Storytellers,** by Caroline Feller Bauer, and **A Storyteller's Choice,** by Eileen Colwell. Both of these books gave good suggestions as well as references for stories to be read aloud.

Once the children had selected their stories, we read them over and over again, both silently and aloud, so as to become genuinely familiar with them. Michelle chose **The Quiet Mother and the Noisy Little Boy,** by Charlotte Zolotow. Melissa chose **All in One Piece,** by Jill Murphy. Robert selected **The Plant Sitter,** by Gene Zion. And Raymond chose **Henry Explores the Jungle,** by Mark Taylor. Then each child decided which portions of their books should be memorized word-for-word. We had many practice sessions in which the children would perform in front of each other. Praise and advice were lovingly offered.

We also used reference books while at the library to gather information about the author for each book chosen. We utilized *Children's Literature Review,* by Block, Riley, and Senick, and *The Who's Who of Children's Literature,* edited by Brian Doyle.

We taped the children reading their stories aloud and let them listen to themselves. Then we taped them giving their story presentation in their own words. This allowed them to hear themselves as others would hear them. This was beneficial; however, they still needed to be able to view themselves as others would view them. So we borrowed a video camera and videotaped the children giving their presentations.

Typing Exercises: The older children typed the entire text of their stories. They also typed parables from the Bible, and we discussed how our Lord used parables, or stories, to teach the people. These passages were from the Gospel of Mark. These parables were read aloud to the younger children.

Dictation: I dictated selected passages from the books the children chose for storytelling. This helped with story familiarization, spelling, and punctuation skills. I also dictated the passages from the front inside book jackets of each of their books, as these capsulized the contents of each book. Portions from the book, *A Storyteller's Choice,* explaining the history of storytelling were also dictated to the children. The younger children did copy work relating to their books at a level appropriate for each of them.

Videos: *Storytelling Volume 3* and *Storytelling Volume 4.* (These videos were checked out at the public library; they were presentations done by professional storytellers.)

Live Performances: Attended the *Young People's Arts Festival* at Ruth Eckerd Hall to view the presentation of "Peter Rabbit and Other Tales," by Beatrix Potter. Attended and participated in the Hillsborough County Storytelling Festival.

Arts and Crafts: Each of the children made a poster advertising his story. Their posters were illustrated with their favorite scenes from the story.

The following unit was created and conducted by Cameron Albert, Jr., a 15-year-old, home-educated student.

MEDIEVAL UNIT

Books Read or Utilized for Reference:

Kings, Bishops, Knights, and Pawns. By Ralph Arnold.

Castles. By Richard Humble.

Simple Heraldry. By Iain Moncreiffe.

Medieval Days and Ways. By Gertrude Hartman.

Men in Armor. By Richard Suskind.

The Knights. By Michael Gibson.

The Medieval Knight. By Martin Windrow.

A Complete Guide to Heraldry. By A.C. Fox-Davies.

The Institutions, Laws, and Ceremonies of the Most Noble Order of the Garter. By Elias Ashmore.

A Guide to Heraldry. By Ottfried Neubecker.

Heraldry of the Royal Families of Europe. By Jiri Louda and Michael Maclagan.

An Encyclopedic Dictionary of Heraldry. By Julian Franklin and John Tanner.

Design Your Own Coat of Arms. By Rosemary Chorzempa.

Mottoes. By George Earlie Shankle.

The Castle in the Attic. By Elizabeth Winthrop.

Heraldry. By Julian Franklin

A Dictionary of Heraldry and Related Subjects. By Colonel A.G. Puttock.

Heraldry. By Walter Buehr.

Knights in Armor. By Shirley Glubok.

The First Book of Medieval Man. By D. Sobol.

The Story of Knights and Armor. By Ernest E. Tucker.

Knights and Castles. By Jonathan Rutland.

Knights of the Crusades. By Jay Williams.

The Knight of the Golden Plain. By Mollie Hunter.

Activities:

Made a full suit of armor out of sheet metal.

Made two surcoats — stitched on a sewing machine.

Made a sword with a wooden handle and metal blade.

Made a wooden shield and painted it.

Designed and made a coat of arms.

Studied insignia and medals of U.S. Armed Forces.

Studied insignia and medals of Boy Scouts.

Prepared for Royal Ranger's Pow Wow consisting of a medieval theme.

Hosted a medieval tournament for boys.

Cam is currently writing and editing a medieval newsletter for boys ages 5 to 8 entitled, *The Crusader,* which is published monthly. The newsletter consists of the following:

Explanations for Code of Chivalry

Various activities, i.e., draw a picture and send it in to newsletter.

History lesson based on medieval theme

Continuing story

Advancements and awards, i.e., badges in Boy Scouts

Certificate for each child's accomplishments

Scripture memory

Question-and-answer section

For subscription information, write to:

Cameron Albert, Jr.

215 W. Hiawatha

Tampa, FL 33604

Sample Unit:

HOUSE-CLEANING UNIT

It takes time to prepare for our unit studies. We often find the house deteriorating about us. How can we find the time to effectively clean our homes and plan our units? First things first, let's get organized.

It is very difficult for me to teach school if my house looks as if it needs to be thoroughly raked out. Reading all those books on organizing your housework is great, but who has the time to implement all those terrific time-saving ideas, teach the children and prepare a decent evening meal? Getting your youngsters to help is definitely the answer, but just how do you set up this routine and teach?

One possibility is to integrate your housework into a unit study. You may already own some of those wonderful how-to-clean-your-house books. But if you don't, have no fear for the library is near. Investigate the children's section as well as the adult section. Choose a plan that works for you, whether it be charts, graphs, calendars, or index cards to help you organize your work. Let each capable child make cards or a notebook with a list of his or her chores. Your charts or graphs can be as detailed as necessary, stating when each job is to be undertaken.

Some jobs require attention less frequently and are, therefore, often neglected entirely. Send your children on a house-cleaning hunt and have them make a list or all the tasks they can envision. Then categorize them according to how often they should be tackled, and determine the length of time needed to complete each job. Perhaps you may also want to rate each job as difficult, moderate or easy, and place age levels by each one.

Office supply stores have large, desk top calendars at very reasonable prices, which are excellent for logging specific chores, especially those undertaken less frequently. A smaller calendar may be purchased or designed and then photocopied for each child, thus enabling them to record their own jobs and any to be jointly tackled. Then as each chore is completed, they can mark it off their calendars. Younger children can use rubber stamps, magazine pictures or their own drawings to represent chores on their calendars. You can choose to fill out an entire year or just a few months at a time. You will be teaching your children valuable life skills, not only in how to clean but in how to organize their lives. Just think how much your children will learn about calendars by using this method. Also, many disputes over who is to do what are squelched in advance since all the information is recorded ahead of time. If the children want to trade jobs occasionally, housework coupons can be issued and exchanged.

How about doing a massive clean-out and hold a garage sale. The money earned can be used to buy household cleaning tools. It is difficult to get enthused about cleaning the house when the mop-head leaves sponge crumbs all over the floor and the vacuum blows out more dust than it takes in. Have your children clip coupons for cleaning products and check ads for the best prices. This helps them to be good stewards of the family's money.

It is necessary to train your children in effective cleaning methods, but it is also beneficial for the older children to train the younger in specific tasks that the older children have already mastered. Character qualities come into play here as the older must be patient with the younger. We also want our children to cheerfully do their work.

Besides making lists of jobs and filling in charts, calendars, or graphs, many other writing skills can be developed. For example, your children can write poems about cleaning. The book *Precious Moments Through the Year Stories* has several clever poems about housework. These can be used as typing exercises. Easily enough, several short stories can be written about housework. Detective or mystery stories seem good choices, i.e., *The Case of the Missing Sock.* Check your library for fictional books pertaining to housework.

Investigate the Bible to see what you can find about neatness and cleanliness. What character qualities should we stress when caring for our homes? Ask your children what they think. Are they thoughtful, considerate, patient, diligent, and trustworthy? What are the fruits of the Spirit? Housework may seem like a lowly job, but as our Messiah humbled Himself and became a servant, He set an example for us to follow.

Once you've developed a house-cleaning routine, you might want to take one day a week and devote your school time to housework. We have found this very effective since everyone knows his job and how to execute it well. This also allows time to train the children in additional jobs once others have been mastered. A house-cleaning unit is a great way to break the ice and cultivate lifelong cleaning habits.

Sample Unit:

COOKING UNIT

Frequently, a mother will remark that she finds it difficult to teach her children and prepare dinner. This is something I struggle with, too. I feel the solution to this problem is to devise a unit study. This unit study involves cooking and can easily be a springboard for many other related studies. For instance, prepare cuisine from different countries and engage in a brief study about these countries at the same time. For an artistic project, create table decorations representing these countries. Math skills are sharpened as you measure and often double recipes. This is an excellent time to learn about cups, pints, quarts, gallons, teaspoons, tablespoons, and other units of measure. Even little ones will have fun using rice or water to fill measuring cups and containers.

Check out various recipe books from the library, both adults' and children's books, and let each child select one that interests him. Discuss nutrition, calories, fat, carbohydrates, and so on. Explore the Bible for insights into health and nutrition. Study the biblical dietary laws and discover how current books on nutrition support them. One helpful book is entitled *God's Key to Health and Happiness,* by Elmer Josephson.

Supply each of your children with an index card box or recipe box filled with plenty of cards. Have each child write or type tested recipes on their cards, being sure to include the golden oldies, but also include new recipes which you have prepared. Each child may be responsible for recording certain recipes, and they can exchange recipes by photocopying them and then gluing them to cards. Encourage your children to write letters to those friends or relatives they choose and ask for their favorite recipes. Recipes can be collected from magazines and newspapers, too. Have your children then categorize them according to kinds of foods.

One method of recipe-card-keeping shared with me by a friend requires a card listing the ingredients needed to make a complete meal. Instructions for preparing the meal are given on a separate card. When planning the meals for a week, remove the ingredient cards and make a grocery list for the necessary items.

Have your older children plan the meals for a week and then help prepare them. Also have them do the grocery shopping, clipping coupons, and checking ads ahead of time. Help them learn to stay within the grocery budget. Select a system for your meal planning, such as scheduling two weeks of evening meals in which no two meals are the same. This schedule can be repeated, substituting optional meals that add variety and allow for experimentation.

Younger children can help plan and prepare a meal. Teach proper care of utensils and safety precautions. Remind them that cleaning up is part of the job.

As an additional writing exercise, have your children create a menu listing and illustrating their favorite foods. They can also make up silly recipes or poems about food. To make their recipe files elaborate, they can photograph various dishes they have prepared. Writing a family cookbook will be a rewarding project for sharing with relatives and friends.

Integrate science in the kitchen by conducting various experiments with different food substances. Jane Hoffman's *Backyard Scientist* books have many pertinent experiments.

Your children can add to their recipe file as they

try new dishes. When they have their own homes, they will already be well prepared for managing meals. Even the boys will find this helpful as their wives are presented with tried and true recipes, and their wives will be pleasantly surprised to find their husbands are capable cooks.

Encourage your children to continue assisting you with the family meal planning and preparation. If you plan it just right, you may only have to spend a few days in the kitchen each week, while the children handle the meals for the remainder of the time. For an exciting unit finale, dine at a restaurant serving foreign cuisine, possibly dressing in foreign attire for the occasion.

Sample Unit:

GREEK AND ROMAN STUDIES

The following unit was submitted to me by Cathy Duffy, author of the *Christian Home Educators' Curriculum Manuals for Elementary Grades and Junior/Senior High.*

I will list the books she feels are most worthwhile. She states that her children read much more than she did, although some books were used by them as a group. Even though some of these books may be out of print and difficult to obtain, she comments that the value of such a list probably is in suggesting types of books to look for.

The Wonderful World of Mathematics, by Lancelot Hogeben; Doubleday and Co., Inc., NY; 1955. Traces the history of mathematics in colorfully illustrated format through major cultures. Extremely interesting.

Archimedes, by Martin Gardner; The Macmillan Co., NY; 1965. Biography of the important Greek mathematician.

Alexander the Great, by John Gunther; Random House, NY; 1953. Well-written biography.

See Inside An Ancient Greek Town, R.J. Unstead; A Grisewood and Dempsey Ltd., London, 1986. Helps with cultural understanding. Well illustrated. It looks like many of the Usborne books, but a little less cluttered.

The Adventures of Odysseus and The Tale of Troy, (Homer) adapted by Padraic Colum; The Macmillan Co., NY; 1918. Fairly easy-to-read version. Excellent for an overview of how gods and goddesses were perceived by the Greeks.

See Inside: A Roman Town, by R.J. Unstead, ed.; Kingfisher Books Ltd., Elsley Court, London; 1986. Further cultural understanding. Well illustrated. It looks like many of the Usborne books, but a little less cluttered.

The Everyday Life of a Roman Soldier, by Giovanni Caselli; Peter Bedrick Books (Distributed by Harper and Row), NY. Heavily and colorfully illustrated. Elementary grades.

Cultural Atlas for Young People: Ancient Rome, by Mike Corbishley; Facts on File, NY; 1989. History, geography, culture, and more is covered in depth with lots of illustrations.

How Should We Then Live?: The Rise and Decline of Western Thought and Culture, by Francis A. Schaeffer; Crossway Books, IL; 1976. The first chapter is specifically about ancient Rome, but the entire book is an excellent study of the interaction of philosophy, religion, art, literature, government, economics, and other major influences in all cultures.

Roman Mythology, by Stewart Perowne; The Hamlyn Publishing Group Ltd., London, England; 1969. Heavily illustrated with photographs of statues, reliefs, mosaics, and paintings of gods and goddesses. It correlates Greek and Roman deities and tells the story of each one.

History of Art, by H.W. Janson; Prentice-Hall, Inc., NJ, and N. Abrams, Inc., NY; 1965. Much history is incorporated into the teaching about art. It puts everything in context in a way that works nicely with Schaeffer's *How Should We Then Live* concept.

Julius Caesar, Shakespeare. We read some of this also.

AN INTRODUCTION TO THE REFERENCE SECTION OF THE CHILDREN'S DEPARTMENT OF THE PUBLIC LIBRARY

In *How to Create Your Own Unit Studies,* I rather briefly described some of the useful books which can be found in the children's reference section of the public library. There are a vast number of books in this section which would be very beneficial in aiding you in the search for materials pertaining to your unit of study. Therefore, I have further researched this section of the library and have compiled a guide naming and describing some of the more useful books. Hopefully, this guide will help acquaint you with the reference section and allow you to choose some of its more useful books without having to monotonously wade through them all.

Since these books cannot be checked out, you must use them while at the library, thus valuable time would be wasted if you had to first search for a particular book to suit your needs and then draw information from it. Naturally, we cannot expect all libraries to have the exact same books in their reference sections, but enough books are listed in the guide that you will most likely find some in your library to suit your needs.

I have listed the call numbers for the reference books to enable you to more easily locate them. Some books I came across in my research I have omitted from this guide. For example, reference guides for books dealing in values clarification.

I have found that a small number of the books found in the children's reference section are also available on the regular shelves and may be checked out. Here again, the call numbers will help you to locate these books. The reference section is basically made up of four kinds of books: general reference books such as dictionaries, atlases, and encyclopedias; books deemed to be of high educational value, such as Newbery Medal Books, Caldecott Medal Books, history books, fairy tales, books on art, and books on music; handbooks for teaching various skills; and guides for locating specific books in the library.

When using the children's reference section of your public library, you will be more successful if you visit the main branch in your library system, as they will have the widest selection of books from which to choose. Remember also to investigate the adult reference section of your library. You may want to find some more challenging books for older students in this section. In smaller libraries, the adults' and children's reference sections are combined. I feel this makes it more difficult to use, but having the call numbers from the reference guide will be helpful.

There are also many good biographies in the adult section which can be read aloud to the older as well as younger children. And of course, there is the fine arts section with its own guides and card catalogue to help you in selecting books to enhance your unit. I use many of the books from the fine arts section as they are useful for their excellent pictures. The quality of the art reproductions found in these books generally surpasses that found in the books in the children's section.

As I began to compile this guide for the reference section of the children's department, I realized it would be impossible for me to review every book. Many of the books are similar in content and it would prove repetitious for me to comment on each one; however, I've tried to include enough so that you may be able to find a sufficient number of them in your library. My main intention for this guide is to expose you to the kinds of resources available that will aid you in developing your unit study. Conducting this research has helped me a great deal to uncover the treasures that are buried in the library.

The library can be a tremendous source for materials if only we can learn how to tap into it. Unfortunately, many Christians feel that the public library is full of secular books, and they want their children to only read "Christian books," thus they miss out on some of the best books ever written. In the first half of this century, many books were written that exemplified Christian principles. And even today there are good books being written that uphold biblical, moral principles, but we often have to search to uncover these gems. This guide will serve its purpose if it acts as an instrument with which to unveil these treasures.

A GENERAL GUIDE TO THE REFERENCE SECTION OF THE CHILDREN'S DEPARTMENT OF THE PUBLIC LIBRARY

THE RANDOM HOUSE DICTIONARY OF THE ENGLISH LANGUAGE: JR423.

MACMILLAN PICTURE DICTIONARY FOR CHILDREN: JR423.

THE LINCOLN WRITING DICTIONARY FOR CHILDREN: JR423. Harcourt, Brace, and Jovanovich.

DOUBLEDAY CHILDREN'S THESAURUS: JR423.1. Very helpful for allowing the children to find an alternative to overused words. Look for this book on the regular shelves under the same catalogue number.

THE COMPLETE RHYMING DICTIONARY: JR427. Edited by Clement Wood. Beneficial for enabling your children to become fine poets. Once again, check the regular shelves for this book.

MOTHER GOOSE BOOKS: You will find a large selection of Mother Goose-type books and other nursery rhyme books. Some of these are catalogued under ER, for easy reader, and are arranged alphabetically according to the author's last name. Others are catalogued under JR398. However, in the reference section, these are all located on the same shelves. This enables you to view these nursery-rhyme-type books at a glance; however, most should be available on the regular shelves.

CALDECOTT MEDAL BOOKS: A large selection of these award books is located here and can usually be found on the regular shelves, but they are consolidated in the reference section to always be available for in-library use. This enables you to become familiarized with these books at a glance. These are catalogued under the author's last name. The Caldecott Medal is awarded each year for the children's book with the most outstanding illustrations.

NEWBERY MEDAL BOOKS: Once again, a large selection of these books is available here for you to examine. Generally, these books are of a high literary quality and make very good read-aloud books. Next time you're looking for a good book to read to your children, try browsing through these. The Newbery Medal is awarded each year for the book published in that year making the greatest contribution to children's literature. Another excellent book is a biography of John Newbery, for whom the Newbery Award is named. It is entitled *Songs for Sixpence,* by Elizabeth Blackstock, and is located in the junior biography section.

CHILDREN'S BOOKS IN PRINT VOL. 1, SUBJECT GUIDE: JR028.52. R.R. Bowker Company. This enables you to find titles of books that pertain to a particular subject. Each subject is listed alphabetically.

CHILDREN'S BOOKS IN PRINT VOL. 1, SUBJECT GUIDE: JR028.52. R.R. Bowker Company. This enables you to find titles of books that pertain to a particular subject. Each subject is listed alphabetically.

CHILDREN'S BOOKS IN PRINT VOL. 2, AUTHORS, TITLES, AND ILLUSTRATORS: JR028.52. R.R. Bowker Company. This is useful for locating other books by an author you are interested in. Remember that just looking in the card catalogue under a particular author will not help you to locate books by that author that may not be in your library. Perhaps another library in the system would have a book you need. You could have the librarian check this in the computer. Or perhaps you liked a particular illustrator and you would like to find out what other books he or she has illustrated. And you may know of a title of a book for which you don't know the author and cannot find this specific book in the card catalogue. This book would be helpful in both cases. This volume also includes children's book awards for 1980-1990.

AUTHORS—BOOKS IN PRINT: JR015. R.R. Bowker Company. This includes all books, not just children's books.

TITLES—BOOKS IN PRINT: JR015. R.R. Bowker Company. See above.

PUBLISHERS BOOKS IN PRINT: JR015. R.R. Bowker Company. This will enable you to locate books by a particular publisher you may favor.

O.P.-O.S.I.—OUT OF PRINT, OUT OF STOCK INDEFINITELY: JR015. R.R. Bowker Company. This will aid you in locating pertinent information about a book you may be interested in but which is out of print. Many times libraries will own copies of books out of print, or specialty used-book stores may be able to track them down for you.

ENCYCLOPEDIAS: All the basic encyclopedia sets are catalogued under JR031. Libraries will vary in their selection of encyclopedias. Looking these volumes over may help you decide which set of encyclopedias you might wish to purchase. You can pick up used sets at yard sales and used-book stores. Those located in the public library we frequent are: *Children's Britannica, Merit Students Encyclopedia, World Book, The New Book of Knowledge* and *Compton's Encyclopedia.*

JR. HIGH SCHOOL LIBRARY CATALOG: JR011. Edited by Juliette Yaakov. This edition includes 3,219 titles accompanied by descriptions, page numbers, date published, and Dewey Decimal Classification for grades seven through nine. An author, title, subject and analytical index makes this easy to use.

HOW TO USE REFERENCE MATERIALS: JR011.02. By Bernice MacDonald.

CHILDREN'S FILMS AND VIDEOS, FILMSTRIPS, AND RECORDINGS, 1973-1986: JR011.37 Assoc. for Library Services to Children.

**REFERENCE BOOKS FOR YOUNG READERS—
AUTHORITATIVE EVALUATIONS OF
ENCYCLOPEDIAS, ATLASES, AND
DICTIONARIES:** JR011.02. By Marion Sader. Buying
guide series. This would be useful to look through
before purchasing any reference materials.

**BEYOND PICTURE BOOKS, A GUIDE TO FIRST
READERS:** JR011.62. By Barbara Barstow and Judith
Riggle.

**BILINGUAL BOOKS IN SPANISH AND ENGLISH
FOR CHILDREN:** JR011.62. By Doris C. Dale.

**CHOICES—A CORE COLLECTION FOR YOUNG
RELUCTANT READERS:** JR011.62. By Burke. I spent
some time looking this one over and think it would be
useful. The author says in the introduction that as she
visited the schools, she found that the reluctant reader
is the rule rather than the exception, and so she compiled this collection of titles and descriptions of
readers for those children. These are books of high
interest on an easier level.

**THE ELEMENTARY SCHOOL PAPERBACK
COLLECTION:** JR011.62. By John T. Gillespie. This
volume includes brief descriptions. Some children prefer reading paperback books. Now many of the classics
are printed in paperback form.

**DEVELOPING LEARNING SKILLS THROUGH
CHILDREN'S LITERATURE—AN IDEA BOOK
FOR K-5 CLASSROOMS AND LIBRARIES:**
JR011.62. By Mildred Knight Laughlin and Letty S.
Watt. This book lists objectives, recommended reading
and activities for each topic. It includes *Winnie the
Pooh,* Laura Ingalls Wilder, Hans Christian Andersen,
and many more that look interesting.

MAGAZINES FOR SCHOOL LIBRARIES: JR011.62.
By Bill Katz. This includes elementary, junior high and
high school libraries. All magazines are arranged by
subjects, including art, birds, comics, education,
health, medicine, military, music and dance, geography,
and more. This book informs you of magazines
specifically related to certain topics. The addresses are
listed as well so you can order particular magazines
that would correspond with a unit you are doing. The
library also carries magazines on various subjects, including back issues.

**OPENING DOORS FOR PRESCHOOL CHILDREN
AND THEIR PARENTS:** JR011.62. By the American
Library Association. Includes books, films, filmstrips,
recordings and toys, and regalia.

**NEWBERY AND CALDECOTT MEDAL AND
HONOR BOOKS AND ANNOTATED
BIBLIOGRAPHY:** JR011.62. By Peterson and Solt.
Lists Newbery Award Books beginning with the first in
1922 through today, and lists Caldecott Medal Books
beginning with 1938 through today. One book is chosen for each award for the year it is published. This
book provides descriptions of each book listed.

MASTER INDEX TO SUMMARIES OF CHILDREN'S BOOKS: JR011.62. By Eloise S. Pettus. Volume I: A-Z, volume II: title and subject indexes. These volumes are to be used together; for example, look up *sewing* in the subject index in volume II and cross reference to volume I for titles, authors, and a description of books concerning sewing.

POETRY ANTHOLOGIES FOR CHILDREN AND YOUNG PEOPLE: JR011.62. By Olexer. Includes author, title, and subject indexes. Descriptions of poems are given along with appropriate grade levels. If you're studying a particular topic, this book can be used to locate poems relating to that topic. For example, if you're studying the Middle Ages and are taking a close look at armor, you would look up "armor" in this book and find a reference for Longfellow's poem, an entire book, entitled *The Skeleton in Armor.*

INTRODUCING BOOKPLOTS 3 — A BOOK TALK GUIDE FOR USE WITH READERS AGES 8-12: JR011.62. By Diane L. Spirt. Contains summaries of various books falling into specific categories, such as: Getting Along in the Family, Making Friends, Developing Values, Forming a View of the World, Respecting Living Creatures, etc. Not only will this book introduce you to books for various ages and of various themes, but it will inform you as to how to introduce these books to your children to cause them to want to read them. It also lists related books and materials such as filmstrips and recordings. This book contains a subject index, helpful for locating books pertaining to your unit of study or to your child's particular interests.

PRIMARY PLOTS — A BOOK TALK GUIDE FOR USE WITH READERS AGES 4-8: JR011.62. By Rebecca L. Thomas. Similar in content to the book listed previously but for use with younger children.

BOOKS FOR CHILDREN TO READ ALONE — A GUIDE FOR PARENTS AND LIBRARIANS, PRE-K THROUGH GRADE 3: JR011.62. By George Wilson and Joyce Moss. This book is very helpful in that it breaks down the books into categories such as: (1) Books for the Beginning Reader: Wordless or Nearly Wordless Books, (2) Books for the First Half of Grade One, and (3) Books for the Second Half of Grade One. This continues through grade three. This book also has a subject index, readability index (i.e., indexed under grade levels such as 1.0 to 1.4 and 1.5 to 1.9), author index, and title index. Each grade level also has further categories such as Easy, Average, and Challenging. By using this book, you can easily put together your own beginning reader series, all from the library. Descriptions are included in many of the books listed.

DOORS TO MORE MATURE READING—DETAILED NOTES ON ADULT BOOKS FOR USE WITH YOUNG PEOPLE: JR016. By Elinor Walker. This book helps familiarize the parent with adult books suitable for use by a teenager. It also lists persons to whom each book will appeal. Unfortunately, this book doesn't have a subject index, but it does have a title index. A big plus is that most of the books reviewed were written before 1950.

ENCYCLOPEDIA BUYING GUIDE: JR016.03. By Kenneth Kister. This book reviews all general English language encyclopedias.

INDEX TO FAIRY TALES: JR016.398.

INDEX TO FAIRY TALES SUPPLEMENT: JR016.398.

INDEX TO FAIRY TALES SECOND SUPPLEMENT: JR016.398. The volumes listed above will prove helpful for locating fairy tales relating to your unit study. For instance, you can look under "A" for "ants" to find an entire page of ant tale listings. You can also use this guide to find fairy tales written by a specific author.

MATHEMATICS LIBRARY—ELEMENTARY AND JUNIOR HIGH SCHOOL: JR016.51. By Clarence E. Hardgrove and Herbert Miller. This slim volume includes books to enrich your math program with brief descriptions of each book.

SUBJECT INDEX GUIDE TO CHILDREN'S PLAYS: JR016.8. American Library Association, Elizabeth D. Briggs, Chairman. "Each entry gives the name of the play, indicates by code number the book in which the play is found, and includes a page reference to the play's location, the grades for which it is suited, the number of characters required, and the number of acts or scenes, or both." Plays are listed alphabetically according to subject, title, and author. Also included are listings of dramatizations from authors' works such as Hans Christian Andersen, and Ingri and Edgar D'Aulaire.

HISTORY IN CHILDREN'S BOOKS—AN ANNOTATED BIBLIOGRAPHY FOR SCHOOLS AND LIBRARIES: JR016.909. By Zena Sutherland. This book is divided into chapters: Primitive and Ancient Times, Africa, Asia, Pacific Regions, Polar and Far North, Europe, Latin America, Canada, Explorers of the New World and the United States, which itself is subdivided into time periods, peoples, and places. It includes biographies, as well as historical fiction and easy readers. You will find a brief description and approximate grade level for each book listed.

AMERICAN HISTORY IN JUVENILE BOOKS—A CHRONOLOGICAL GUIDE: JR016.973. By Seymour Metzner. This book lists biographies, fiction, nonfiction, and approximate grade levels; however, it does not give a description of the books listed.

**THE PICTURE FILE—A MANUAL AND
CURRICULUM-RELATED SUBJECT HEADING
LIST:** JR025.34. By Donna Hill. Tells how to create
and use a picture file to enhance a curriculum. Gives
ideas on how to locate free-of-charge pictures from
various sources. It appears this book can be used for a
family project to create a picture file for a specific
unit.

**BOOKSHARING, 101 PROGRAMS TO USE WITH
PRESCHOOLERS:** JR027.62. By Margaret
MacDonald. Includes books, songs and activities all
centered around a particular theme.

**MUSICAL STORY HOURS—USING MUSIC WITH
STORYTELLING AND PUPPETRY:** JR027.62. By
William M. Painter. Suggests books to read aloud with
music and activities to go with the stories. Many of
the records and books can be found in larger libraries.

THE FLANNEL BOARD STORYTELLING BOOK:
JR027.6251. By Judy Sierra. Includes entire story text,
poems, songs and over 250 accompanying reproducible
patterns.

JUNIOR PLOTS: JR028.1. By Gillespie and Lembo.
Lists books with their descriptions for young adults.

**SUBJECT AND TITLE INDEX TO SHORT STORIES
FOR CHILDREN:** JR028.5. Compiled by the
American Library Association, chairman Julia Carter.
Lists books by subject and title but does not include
descriptions of books.

BOOKS FOR CHILDREN: JR028.5. Compiled by the
American Library Association. Lists books under
various categories: Art, History, Geography, Science,
Biographies, etc. Also gives descriptions of books.

CHILDREN'S LITERATURE REVIEW: JR028.5. Compiled by Block, Riley, and Senick. This set contains
many volumes consisting of general commentaries
about individual authors and many of their books.
These volumes would prove beneficial for a study of a
particular author and his or her works. Each volume is
alphabetically arranged according to the author's last
name. Each volume contains a listing of authors from
A-Z; therefore, Volume I may not contain Lewis Car-
roll, but he is included in Volume II. Indexes are included so that you may quickly locate the volume
needed for a particular author. These volumes allow
you to get a feel for an author and some of his books
at a glance. My library has 21 volumes.

CHILDREN'S BOOKS: AWARDS AND PRIZES:
JR028.5. By the Children's Book Council, Inc. Prizes
and awards for young adult books are also included in
this book. It is divided into the following categories:
U.S. Awards Selected by Adults, U.S. Awards Selected
by Young Readers, British Commonwealth Awards, and
International and Multinational Awards. Over 100 separate book awards and their recipients through 1985
are contained in this book. A description of each
award is also given.

THE WHO'S WHO OF CHILDREN'S LITERATURE: JR028.5. Compiled and edited by Brian Doyle. Contains over 400 names with biographical, bibliographical, and background details covering a selection of British, Continental European, and American authors from 1800 to the present day. Very good for studying particular authors.

PICTURE BOOKS FOR CHILDREN: JR028.5. By Patricia J. Cianciolo. A guide to children's picture books with descriptions of books included.

THE BOOK FINDER: JR028.5. By Sharon S. Dreyer. "Helps you match books to the needs and problems of children and young people." You'll find volumes with selections of books published from different years. Books are categorized according to theme, for example: Accidents, Adoption, Anger, Bedtime, Belonging, etc. Some categories are undesirable, but others are very useful.

TREASURE FOR THE TAKING—A BOOK LIST FOR BOYS AND GIRLS: JR028.5. By Anne T. Eaton. Includes categories such as Talking Beasts and Other Creatures, Trees and Flowers, Ships and the Sea, Legends and Hero Tales, Stories With Historical Background, What To Do, and How To Do It. Descriptions are included for each book.

BEST BOOKS FOR CHILDREN—PRESCHOOL THROUGH GRADE SIX: JR028.5. By John Gillespie and Corinne Nade. Major subjects are arranged alphabetically. Contains descriptions of each book listed and has a subject/grade-level index.

SPORTS BOOKS FOR CHILDREN: JR028.5. By Barbara Harrah. Includes book descriptions and books are arranged alphabetically by sport subjects.

STORY STRETCHERS: JR028.5. By Shirley Raines and Robert Canady. "Activities to expand children's favorite books." Probably for preschool through third grade.

BASIC COLLECTION OF CHILDREN'S BOOKS IN SPANISH: JR028.5. By Isabel Schon. Contains a subject and title index.

A TO ZOO—SUBJECT ACCESS TO CHILDREN'S PICTURE BOOKS: JR028.5. By Carolyn W. Lima. Alphabetically arranged according to topic. Contains descriptions of books.

CALDECOTT MEDAL BOOKS 1938-1957: JR028.5. Edited by B.M. Miller. Contains artists' acceptance papers, their biographies, and a critical analysis by Esther Averill: "What is a picture book?"

NEWBERY MEDAL BOOKS 1922-1955: JR028.5. Edited by B.M. Miller and E.W. Field. Contains authors' acceptance papers, biographies of award winners, and appraisals of winning books.

NEWBERY AND CALDECOTT MEDAL BOOKS, 1966-1975: JR028.5079. Edited by Kingman. Same format as previously listed books.

NEWBERY AND CALDECOTT MEDAL BOOKS, 1976-1985: JR028.0579. Edited by Kingman. Same format as above. (Note: There are probably other books for the years omitted. Also note the listing I made earlier for the *Newbery and Caldecott Medal and Honor Books, an Annotated Bibliography* by Solt. This covers all the years but doesn't include all the same information as these books listed above.)

ADVENTURING WITH BOOKS, A BOOKLIST FOR PRE K–GRADE 6: JR028.5. Edited by Diane Monson. Includes categories such as Books for Young Children, Traditional Literature, Modern Fantasy, Historical Fiction, Contemporary Realistic Fiction, Poetry, Language, Social Studies, Biography, Sciences, Fine Arts, Crafts and Hobbies, etc. Each category is further divided. Each book listed includes appropriate grade levels, number of pages, and a description.

CHOOSING BOOKS FOR KIDS—CHOOSING THE RIGHT BOOK FOR THE RIGHT CHILD AT THE RIGHT TIME—OVER 1500 BOOK REVIEWS: JR028.5. Edited by William Hooks. Includes divisions such as books for Babies, Toddlers, Three- and Four-Year-Olds, Books for Fives, Books for Sixes and Sevens, Books for Eights and Nines, and Books for Ten- to Twelve-Year-Olds.

CELEBRATING WITH BOOKS: JR028.5. By Polette and Hamlin. A review of books dealing with holiday themes.

BOOKS FOR BOYS AND GIRLS, A STANDARD WORK OF REFERENCE FOR LIBRARIANS: JR028.5. Edited by Mary Bagshaw. "Each book is fully annotated and the list is arranged by subject according to the child's reading interests. Books chosen include only those considered to be of permanent interest to boys and girls."

TWENTIETH CENTURY CHILDREN'S WRITERS: JR028.5. Edited by Daniel Kirkpatrick. Contains biographies, bibliographies, and critical essays detailing each writer's influences.

WORLD HISTORY IN JUVENILE BOOKS: JR028.52. By Metzner. Books are categorized by country. Each division includes biographies, fiction, and nonfiction. The title, author, number of pages, and grade level are given, but descriptions are not included.

EUROPEAN HISTORICAL FICTION AND BIOGRAPHIES FOR CHILDREN AND YOUNG PEOPLE: JR028.52. By Jeanette Hotchkiss. Categorized by country and then further divisions such as General History, Myths and Legends, and specific centuries are included. Contains descriptions of each book.

AMERICAN HISTORICAL FICTION AND BIOGRAPHIES FOR CHILDREN AND YOUNG PEOPLE: JR028.52. By Jeanette Hotchkiss. Divided into time periods such as Early Explorations, Colonial Period, Revolutionary Period, etc. Also categorized according to subject such as The Arts, Folklore, Industry and Technology, Science, etc. Includes description of each book.

AUTHORS OF BOOKS FOR YOUNG PEOPLE: JR028.5. By Ward and Marquardt. Includes biographical information on children's authors.

THE ELEMENTARY SCHOOL LIBRARY COLLECTION—A GUIDE TO BOOKS AND OTHER MEDIA: JR028.52. The Brodart Company. Contains a subject guide and lists authors, titles and descriptions of books. Includes fiction, non-fiction, and easy.

YANKEE DOODLE'S LITERARY SAMPLER OF PROSE, POETRY, AND PICTURES: JR028.52. By V. Haviland and M. Coughlan. "Being an Anthology of Diverse Works Published for the Edification and/or Entertainment of Young Readers in America before 1900." You can use this to give your children a glimpse of the past. This book is not a guide to other books, but rather is a sampling of books of long ago.

YOUNG PEOPLE'S LITERATURE IN SERIES— FICTION, NON-FICTION, AND PUBLISHER SERIES: JR028.52. By Rosenburg. Includes lists of authors and their works included in a series. Gives an overview of the content of the series and lists appropriate grade levels. Many young children are encouraged to continue reading if they are exposed to books within a series.

CHILDHOOD IN POETRY: JR028.52. By John Mackay Shaw. A multivolumed set consisting of a catalogue with biographical and critical annotations of the books of English and American poets. This is categorized according to the author's last name, but also includes indexes composed of the author's last name and subject headings. Therefore, you can find poems relating to a specific topic or other poems by a particular author. Also included are typical passages of the poems. I have found that these books tend to be difficult to use because many of the poems listed are not easily found in the library. If you don't have much success with this set, select a large poetry volume with a subject index and locate poems dealing with your topic. An author index will probably be included in this poetry volume as well for locating poems by a particular author.

CREATIVE ENCOUNTERS—ACTIVITIES TO EXPAND CHILDREN'S RESPONSES TO LITERATURE: JR028.55. By A. Polkingham and C. Toohey. Includes activities to be utilized with various books for young children. Some of the books selected are: *If the Dinosaurs Came Back, The Princess and the Pea, Harold and the Purple Crayon, Corduroy, A Pocket for Corduroy,* and *A Color of His Own.*

PROGRAMMING FOR SCHOOL AGE CHILD CARE— A CHILDREN'S LITERATURE BASED GUIDE: JR028.5. By Melba Hawkins. Contains ideas for integrating children's literature with creative art activities, creative dramatics, creative music activities, cooking experiences, and special days of the year. Book reviews are given along with suggested activities. Although the title indicates that this book is for child care, the book looks very interesting.

THIS WAY TO BOOKS: JR028.55. By Caroline Bauer. Contains hundreds of ideas and programs designed to get children and books together. The methods described here include the use of toys, puppets, crafts, music, costumes, and banners as devices to unite children and books. The ideas are very interesting and creative.

THE 1991 INFORMATION PLEASE ALMANAC: JR031 HOUGHTON MIFFLIN COMPANY. Contains information on business and economy, taxes, first aid, nutrition and health, geography and an atlas, and much more. There are also several other almanacs, including almanacs for children.

A FIRST DICTIONARY OF CULTURAL LITERACY— WHAT OUR CHILDREN NEED TO KNOW: JR031.02. By E.D. Hirsch, Jr. Written in response to the outcry that our children today are suffering educationally. This book is interesting to browse through; however, it contains only snippets of information.

THE MACMILLAN BOOK OF GREEK GODS AND HEROS: JR292. By Alice Low, illustrated by Arvis Stewart. Includes popular myths and legends. Written in a simplified style and beautifully illustrated.

D'AULAIRES' BOOK OF GREEK MYTHS: JR292. By Ingri and Edgar Parin d'Aulaire. The D'Aulaires are known for their many wonderfully illustrated biographies which are considered children's classics. As Caldecott Award-winning artists, they have written and illustrated one of the most captivating books on Greek myths. The reference section includes other exquisitely illustrated books on GREEK, ROMAN, CELTIC, RUSSIAN, INDIAN, and VIKING MYTHOLOGY and LEGENDS.

THE GOLDEN BIBLE ATLAS WITH RELIEF MAPS IN FULL COLOR: JR220.9. By Samuel Terrien. This book makes an historical and pictorial progression through the Bible written in a style that's understandable for young and old.

BIBLE ENCYCLOPEDIA FOR CHILDREN: JR220.3. By Denis Wrigley. This easy-to-read, fully illustrated text describes the people, main events, places, and leading ideas of the Bible.

THE JUNIOR JEWISH ENCYCLOPEDIA: JR296.03. Edited by Naomi Ben-Asher and Hayim Leaf. An illustrated reference guide covering Jewish life and culture from ancient times to the present.

BLACK STUDIES - A BIBLIOGRAPHY: JR301.45196. By Leonard Irwin. Includes: The History of the Black Experience in America, Biography, Memoirs, Autobiography, Essays, Anthologies, Literature, Music and Arts, and African Background and History. Gives brief reviews of each book listed.

CAREER DISCOVERY ENCYCLOPEDIA: JR331.702. Ferguson Publishing Company. A multivolumed set. "The Career Discovery Encyclopedia is written especially for younger readers. It is designed to enable them and to encourage them to begin learning and thinking about the kinds of jobs and careers that will be available to them as adults." It contains information about more than 500 different kinds of jobs, presented in the form of short articles, no longer than two pages. Each article explains different aspects of the job: what it is like, what kind of education and training are required, what the salary and future prospects for the job are like, and how to get more information.

ACCEPT ME AS I AM—BEST BOOKS OF JUVENILE NONFICTION ON IMPAIRMENTS AND DISABILITIES: JR362.4016. By Friedberg, Mullins, Sukiennik. Categorizes books according to: Physical Problems, Sensory Problems, Cognitive and Behavior Problems, Multiple/Severe and Various Disabilities. This book also includes a subject index. Each book listed receives a half-page to full-page review.

BASIC MEDIA SKILLS THROUGH GAMES: JR371.3078. By Irene Wood Bell and Jeanne E. Wieckert. This book is to familiarize students with the skills necessary to effectively use instructional materials. Although intended for use in a school library, many of these games could be adapted for home use in learning to locate information by using dictionaries, encyclopedias, atlases, tables of contents, and indexes. You can also create your own library at home and make author, title, and subject cards for library books you've checked out, have the children alphabetize their cards and shelve the library books according to their call numbers. Many library skills can be learned at home. My children love playing library and even put slips of paper in the backs of the books and stamp them.

FELT BOARD FUN—FOR EVERYDAY AND HOLIDAYS: JR371.33. By Liz and Dick Wilmes. Includes units describing a variety of activities. Patterns for each unit are included and can be photocopied right at the library. You can let your children cut out the patterns you copy, color them and put them together while engaging in an activity described by the book. There's a good possibility that you will find this book on the regular shelves.

ACTIVE LEARNING—GAMES TO ENHANCE ACADEMIC ABILITIES: JR371.332. By Bryant Cratty. Includes activities for these categories: Calming Down and Tuning Up, Geometric Figures, Remembering Things, Numbers and Counting, Mathematics, Letters, Letter Sounds and Spelling, Reading, and Improving Coordination. The appropriate age is listed for each activity, and some activities are for children up to twelve years old.

MUDPIES TO MAGNETS—A PRESCHOOL SCIENCE CURRICULUM: JR372.35. By R. Williams, R. Rockwell and E. Sherwood. A collection of science activities involving: Construction and Measurement, Scientific Art, Health and Nutrition, Outdoor Science, Creativity and Movement, and more. This would be appropriate for the early grades as well. You could copy a few activities you are interested in. There are several other books for science activities. It is good to check in the reference section as many of these activity books are not found on the regular shelves.

MORE WINDOWS TO THE WORLD—A GOOD APPLE ACTIVITY BOOK FOR GRADES 2-8: JR372.83. By Nancy Everix. This book allows your children to take a trip around the world through hands-on activities. Also includes addresses for the international tourist offices of many countries, enabling you to write for free or inexpensive materials. Here again, desired activities can be photocopied.

Other useful books that I may not have included are handbooks on: STORYTELLING, PUPPETRY, COSTUMES from around the world and from various historical periods, FESTIVALS and ANNUAL EVENTS, FOLKLORE, FAIRY TALES, FABLES, LEGENDS, and FOLKTALES. I have included some specific books, however, that fall into some of these categories. Also you'll find BOY SCOUT, CUB SCOUT, BROWNIE, and GIRL SCOUT HAND-BOOKS. These books are catalogued between JR369 and JR398.

ONCE UPON A TIME—A STORYTELLING HANDBOOK: JR372.64. By Lucille and Bren Breneman. "A study of the techniques of storytelling as an artform useful to teachers, librarians, enter-tainers, speakers, and those in the helping professions."

STORYTELLING—PROCESS AND PRACTICE: JR372.64. By Norma Liro and Sandra Rietz.

THE COMPLETE ANDERSEN: JR398. Translated and edited by Jean Hersholt. "All of the stories of Hans Christian Andersen collected into one volume for the first time. Some never before translated into English and some never before published."

THE STANDARD DICTIONARY OF FOLKLORE: JR398. Funk and Wagnalls. Comprising two volumes that exhibit a major overall survey of world folklore, mythology, and legend.

GRIMM'S TALES FOR YOUNG AND OLD—THE COMPLETE STORIES: JR398. Newly translated by Ralph Manheim.

THE OXFORD DICTIONARY OF NURSERY RHYMES: JR398. Edited by Iona and Peter Opie. Contains more than 500 rhymes and songs and studies their individual histories.

THE FABLES OF AESOP: JR398.2. Rand McNally. Illustrated by Frank Baber.

THE NEW ENCYCLOPEDIA OF SCIENCE: JR500. Raintree Publishers.

NATURE ATLAS OF AMERICA: JR500. By Roland Clement.

ILLUSTRATED LIBRARY OF NATURE: JR500.9. H.S. Stuttman Co., Inc., Pub.

THE MUSEUM OF SCIENCE AND INDUSTRY— BASIC LIST OF CHILDREN'S SCIENCE BOOKS: JR501.6. American Library Association. Includes reviews of books arranged alphabetically according to subject.

THE BEST SCIENCE BOOKS FOR CHILDREN: JR501.6. Edited by Wolff, Fritsche, Gross, and Todd. Includes a subject index and reviews of each book listed.

COMPTON'S DICTIONARY OF NATURAL SCIENCE: JR503.

COMPTON'S ILLUSTRATED SCIENCE DICTIONARY: JR503.

GROWING UP WITH SCIENCE: JR503. H.S. Stuttman Pub. An illustrated encyclopedia of science comprising twenty-five volumes.

RAND McNALLY MATHEMATICS ENCYCLOPEDIA: JR510.3.

THE INTERNATIONAL WILDLIFE ENCYCLOPEDIA: JR510.3. Marshall Cavendish Corporation. Twenty volumes.

THE BIRDS OF AMERICA: JR598.2. By John James Audubon.

You'll find many other ENCYCLOPEDIAS pertaining to ANIMALS, PLANTS, and the SEA. You will find books on HORSES, DOGS, CATS, and other PETS catalogued under JR636.

GARDENER'S ART THROUGH THE AGES: JR709. By de la Croix Tansey.

THE GOLDEN ENCYCLOPEDIA OF ART: JR709. By Eleanor C. Munro.

THE PANTHEON STORY OF ART FOR YOUNG PEOPLE: JR709. By Batterberry. Well written and contains excellent photos of artwork.

THE ART OF BEATRIX POTTER: JR741.6. With notes by Enid and Leslie Linder.

THE RANDOLPH CALDECOTT TREASURY: JR741.6. Edited by Elizabeth Billington.

Other books on famous illustrators can be found in this section also.

A PICTORIAL HISTORY OF MUSIC: JR780.9. By Paul Henry and Otto Bettmann. "The Pageant of Music History presented with more than 600 pictures and an authoritative text."

Other books pertaining to music are catalogued from JR780 to JR784.

Books relating to SPORTS and GAMES are catalogued under JR793.

PRESENTING READER'S THEATER—PLAYS AND POEMS TO READ ALOUD: JR792.0226. By C.F. Bauer.

WRITING WITH PICTURES—HOW TO WRITE AND ILLUSTRATE CHILDREN'S BOOKS: JR808.068. By Uri Shulevitz.

SUBJECT INDEX TO POETRY FOR CHILDREN AND YOUNG PEOPLE: JR808.8. American Library Association. Allows you to locate poems pertaining to a particular topic and uses a cross-reference system to enable you to find the title of a book that a specific poem is published in.

INDEX TO CHILDREN'S POETRY: JR808.8. By John and Sara Brewton. The poems listed are classified by subject. A cross-reference system is used to locate books in which these poems appear. The front of this index, and the one listed above, explain how each of these books is to be used. Only a few minutes are needed to familiarize yourself with these books. You will find indexes for various years available, although authors may vary and the books for different years may appear under different catalogue numbers.

THE SCOTT FORESMAN ANTHOLOGY OF CHILDREN'S LITERATURE: JR808.89. By Zena Sutherland and Mira Livingston. This anthology of children's literature introduces the work of fine authors, new and old, as well as introducing the broad spectrum of contemporary and traditional literature. The material in this book has been divided into three main parts: An Invitation to Poetry, An Invitation to Folklore and Fantasy, and An Invitation to Fiction and Fact. Great as a read-aloud book as it encompasses many variations of children's literature for all ages. This book is often found on the regular shelves of the library as well. There are many books in the reference section to be found pertaining to children's poetry.

VALUES IN SELECTED CHILDREN'S BOOKS OF FICTION AND FANTASY: JR809.39. By C. Field and J. Weiss. "Here are over 700 annotations of books for children from the preschool level to the eighth grade, categorized by ten values they represent or reinforce. The books are culled from titles likely to be in school and public libraries and published in the United States between 1930 and 1984." The titles are divided by age level. Categories of values include: Cooperation, Courage, Friendship and Love of Animals, Friendship and Love of People, Humaneness, Ingenuity, Loyalty, Maturity, Responsibility, and Self-Respect. I recognize many of the titles listed and am pleased overall with the book.

NAME THAT BOOK: JR809.8928. By Janet Greeson and Karen Taha. From primary through junior high. Includes titles, authors and descriptions of books along with

pertinent questions for each book. Apparently, this book has been used by librarians and teachers to play a game called "Battle of Books," which has been played in schools and libraries since 1940. You could use this book and locate books in it you've already read, or choose books listed that you would like to read, and have your own "Battle of Books" game at home. It sounds like great fun. You could even integrate a new aspect and call it "Name that Author."

YESTERDAY'S AUTHORS OF BOOKS FOR CHILDREN: JR809.89. Edited by Anne Commire. Two volumes containing facts and pictures about authors and illustrators of books for young people from early times to 1960.

PRIZE-WINNING BOOKS FOR CHILDREN: JR813.009. By Jacqueline Weiss. "It is the only known review of children's literature based exclusively on prizewinners, a logical source for those who want to read what has been judged as the best." Arranged under various themes, inclusive of descriptions and appropriate age categories. Contains author and title index.

THE FLORIDA HANDBOOK—FLORIDA'S PEOPLE AND THEIR GOVERNMENT: JR917.59. By Allen Morris.

Several other books are included in this section pertaining to FLORIDA. (Each library will have books representative of its state.) Also there are books on LANDS AND PEOPLES, EARLY AMERICAN LIFE, and a variety of ATLASES. These books are catalogued under the numbers 910 to 917.

THE LOOK-IT-UP BOOK OF PRESIDENTS: JR920. By Wyatt Blassingame.

Other books on the PRESIDENTS are in this same area.

FOURTH BOOK OF JUNIOR AUTHORS AND ILLUSTRATORS: JR920. Edited by Montreville and Crawford. Also The Junior Book of Authors, More Junior Authors, and The 3rd Book of Junior Authors. These books include biographical sketches of various authors, while the fourth book also includes illustrators.

ILLUSTRATORS OF CHILDREN'S BOOKS: JR920. Published by Horn Book Incorporated. Includes biographical sketches of various illustrators.

CHILDREN'S AUTHORS AND ILLUSTRATORS: JR920. Edited by Adele Sarkissian. An index to biographical dictionaries. "Provides quick and easy access to biographical information on approximately 20,000 persons found in more than 275 reference books." Useful for a study of children's literature.

INDEX TO COLLECTIVE BIOGRAPHIES FOR YOUNG READERS—ELEMENTARY AND JUNIOR HIGH LEVEL: JR920. By Judith Silverman. This book is divided into two sections, Alphabetical Listings of Biographies and Subject Listings of Biographies. The Alphabetical Listings of Biographies includes brief descriptions of each biographee, for example, baseball player, evangelist, dancer, and so on. The most helpful section of this book, however, is the Subject Listing of Biographies. By using this part of the book, you can locate persons relating to your particular topic or theme. For instance, if you're studying composers, you'll find listings for composers under headings such as American, Austrian, Czech, English, French, Italian, and so on. The birth and death dates are listed for each composer, enabling you to focus on a particular time period as well as on a particular nationality. You'll find lists of persons under authors, engineers, explorers, mathematicians, pianists, and many more. This index enables you to locate a biography on persons relating to most any topic. A cross-reference system is used to locate the books in which each person is depicted.

PEOPLE IN BOOKS: JR920.02. By Margaret Nicholsen. "A Selective Guide to Biographical Literature Arranged by Vocations and Other Fields of Reader Interest." I believe this book is easier to use than *Collective Biographies for Young Readers* in that no cross-reference system is needed to find book titles. You locate a particular topic such as abolitionists, authors, lawyers, physicists, or taxidermists, and the biographees' names are listed along with the titles of their biographies. The names of the authors, publishers, years published, and birth and death dates of the biographees are also included. After finding a person who fits your studies, it is advisable to check the adult section of your library for a biography of that person. I have sometimes found more interesting biographies in the adult section.

INDEX TO SHORT BIOGRAPHIES FOR ELEMENTARY AND JUNIOR HIGH GRADES: JR920.0016. Compiled by Ellen J. Stanius. This book contains a straight alphabetical listing of biographees. It does not include a subject index, detracting from its usefulness. It is helpful to use once you have located the name of a person whom you wish to study, perhaps through consulting *Collective Biographies for Young Readers* or *People in Books,* but possibly you would like a simpler biography about that person. This *Index to Short Biographies* enables you to locate that particular person and thus a short biography title. If you find that your library doesn't have any of the titles you are looking for, have the librarian check to see if another branch owns one. Also, once you have located the name of a person related to your study, you can often find in the junior biography section of your library a book written about that person, as these books are alphabetized according to the biographee's last name.

The reference section also includes books on AMERICAN INDIANS, FRONTIER LIVING, FLORIDA, and UNITED STATES HISTORY; these are catalogued from 970 to 975.

THE RAINBOW BOOK OF AMERICAN HISTORY: JR973. By Earl S. Miers and illustrated by James Daugherty. Contains superb illustrations and an easy-to-follow text written in a story-type fashion. This book is usually found on the regular bookshelves as well, and is one of my favorites.

It is my hope this brief reference guide will have sparked your interest enough to encourage you to take a closer look at what your library has to offer. Make it known to your librarians that you home-educate your children and that the library is a valuable resource to your family. If there are books listed in this guide that you believe would benefit your studies but are not owned by your library system, inform your librarian. I feel that the more we let our needs and interests be known, the sooner the public libraries will stand up and take notice. Find out, too, if you can have a voice in the purchasing of books for your county. I have found most librarians more than willing to help home educators. It is important, as well, that we teach our children how to use the reference section and also help them recognize the other services provided by the public library. You will do well to check out a book explaining the various services and systems the library makes available and utilizes.

The next section comprises an overview of the Dewey Decimal Classification System that divides all non-fiction books into ten groups and further divides each group. Fiction books are arranged alphabetically by the author's last name and appear in a separate section of the library. The children's section of the library is arranged like the adult section; only a "J" for "Juvenile" precedes the call number. An "easy reading" section of books is also available for beginning readers and picture books are available for younger children. Both these sections are arranged by author.

000-099 GENERAL WORKS
010 Bibliographies and Catalogues
020 Library and Information Sciences
030 General Encyclopedic Works
050 General Serial Publications
060 General Organizations, Museums
070 Journalism, Publishing, Newspapers
080 General Collections
090 Manuscripts and Book Rarities

100-199 PHILOSOPHY AND RELATED DISCIPLINES
110 Metaphysics
120 Knowledge, Purpose, Man
130 Popular and Parapsychology, Occultism
140 Specific Philosophical Viewpoints
150 Psychology
160 Logic
170 Ethics
180 Ancient, Medieval, Oriental
190 Modern Western Philosophy

200-299 RELIGION
210 Natural Religion
220 Bible
230 Christian Doctrinal Theology
240 Christian Moral and Devotional
250 Local Church, Religious Orders
260 Social, Ecclesiastical Theology
270 History and Geography of Church
280 Christian Denominations, Sects
290 Other Religions and Comparative

300-399 THE SOCIAL SCIENCES
310 Statistics
320 Political Science
330 Economics
340 Law
350 Public Administration
360 Social Pathology and Services
370 Education
380 Commerce
390 Customs and Folklore

400-499 LANGUAGE
410 Linguistics
420 English, Anglo-Saxon
430 Germanic Languages, German
440 French, Provençal, Catalan
450 Italian, Romanian, Romanic
460 Spanish and Portuguese
470 Italic Languages, Latin
480 Helenic, Classical Greek
490 Other Languages

500-599 PURE SCIENCES
510 Mathematics
520 Astronomy and Allied Sciences
530 Physics
540 Chemistry and Allied Sciences
550 Earth and Other Worlds
560 Paleontology
570 Life Sciences
580 Botanical (Plant Life)
590 Zoological (Animal Life)

600-699 TECHNOLOGY (APPLIED SCIENCES)
610 Medical Sciences
620 Engineering, Allied Operations
630 Agriculture and Related
640 Home Economics
650 Managerial Services
660 Chemical and Related
670 Manufactures
680 Misc. Manufactures
690 Buildings

700-799 THE ARTS
710 Civic and Landscape Art
720 Architecture
730 Plastic Arts, Sculpture
740 Drawing, Decorative and Minor
750 Painting and Paintings
760 Graphic Arts, Prints
770 Photography and Photographs
780 Music
790 Recreational and Performing Arts

800-899 LITERATURE
810 American Literature in English
820 English and Anglo-Saxon Literature
830 Literature of Germanic Languages
840 French, Provençal, Catalan
850 Italian, Romanian, Romanic
860 Spanish and Portuguese Literature
870 Italic Languages Literature, Latin
880 Helenic Languages Literature
890 Literatures of Other Languages

900-999 GENERAL GEOGRAPHY AND HISTORY
910 General Geography, Travel
920 Biography, Genealogy, Insignia
930 Gen. History of Ancient World
940 Gen. History of Europe
950 Gen. History of Asia
960 Gen. History of Africa
970 Gen. History of N. America
980 Gen. History of S. America
990 General History of Other Areas

DEAR READER

This book was developed as a result of the frequent questions I receive concerning unit studies and teaching my children in general. If it weren't for those determined mothers seeking better and more practical methods for teaching their children, I probably would not have written this book.

It is very frustrating for me to see parents struggle through a curriculum only to find the curriculum doesn't meet their needs. The parents are unhappy and the children are even more displeased.

Educating our children doesn't have to be a complicated process, it just needs to be a thoughtful process. Evaluate your priorities and let those priorities be your guide.

I encourage you to send me your comments and questions. This enables me to stay in contact with the needs and interests of home-educating families. I am always looking for good teaching tips myself. I appreciate your input.

Those mothers who were most persistent in their questions will find our conversations between the pages of this book. I offer my thanks to you as you continue to be an encouragement to me.

Please address any comments or questions to:

Valerie Bendt
333 Rio Vista Ct.
Tampa, FL 33604

Thank you!

ABOUT THE AUTHOR

Valerie is the wife of Bruce Bendt and mother of their five children, Michelle, Melissa, Robert, Raymond, and Mandy. Valerie and Bruce have home-educated their children from birth. Bruce is a Bible teacher and pastor of a home church fellowship. He also co-hosts a radio talk show entitled "Battle Lines."

Valerie and Bruce are available to speak on a variety of topics pertinent to home education. For workshop information, write to:

Bendt Family Ministries
333 Rio Vista Ct.
Tampa, FL 33604

FOOTNOTES

1. *American Dictionary of the English Language,* Noah Webster 1828, republished in facsimile edition by the Foundation for American Christian Education, San Francisco, California.

2. *Ibid.*

3. *Webster's Encyclopedia of Dictionaries, New American Edition,* Ottenheimer Pub., Inc., 1978, p. 121.

4. *Webster's New World Dictionary of the American Language,* The World Publishing Co., 1988, p. 444.

5. Susan Schaeffer Macaulay, *For the Children's Sake,* Crossway Books, 1984, p. 8.

6. *Ibid,* p. 82.

7. Philippians 4:8, *New American Standard Version.*

8. Charlotte Mason, *Home Education,* Tyndale House Pub., Inc., 1989. Originally published by Kegan Paul, Trench, Trubner and Co., Ltd., London, England, 1935. p. 153.

9. *For the Children's Sake, Op. cit.,* p. 112.

10. *Home Education, Op. cit.,* p. 98, 99.

11. Ruth Beechick, *You Can Teach Your Child Successfully,* Arrow Press, 1988, p. 297.

12. *Ibid,* p. vii.

13. Donald Graves and Virginia Stuart, *Write From the Start,* NAL PENGUIN, INC., 1985, p. 231.

14. *Home Education, Op. cit.,* p. 80.

15. Franky Schaeffer, *Addicted to Mediocrity,* Crossway Books, 1981, p. 39, 40.

16. Recorded by Sandi Patti, words and music by Phil McHugh and Greg Nelson, *That's the Love of God,* River Oaks Music Co., 1989.

17. James 1:5, *New American Standard Version.*

RESOURCES

The materials I have referred to in this book are listed here with appropriate addresses. I suggest that you write to each company for a catalog.

AMPERSAND PRESS
691 26th Street
Oakland, CA 94612

Games: *O'Euclid, Kril, AC-DC,* and more.

ARISTOPLAY
P.O. Box 7529
Ann Arbor, MI 48107

Games: *Where in the World? Music Maestro II, The Game of Great Composers, Art Deck, Somebody, Hail to the Chief, Made for Trade, Constellation Station, Land Ho!/Tierra Tierra!,* and more.

AUDIO MEMORY PUBLISHING
1433 E. 9th Street
Long Beach, CA 90813

Audio cassettes: *Geography Songs, More Geography Songs,* & many other tapes.

BACKYARD SCIENTIST
Jane Hoffman
P.O. Box 16966
Irvine, CA 92713

Science experiment books.

BENDT FAMILY MINISTRIES
333 Rio Vista Court
Tampa, FL 33604

Hundred Board Activities, by Valerie Bendt.

CHRISTIAN LIFE WORKSHOPS
P.O. Box 2250
Gresham, OR 97030
(503) 667-3942

The Right Choice -- Home Schooling, by Chris Klicka, *The Homeschooling Workshop Cassette Tape Series,* by Gregg Harris. Attend The Homeschooling Workshop nearest you. Write for workshop itinerary.

CLASSIC PLAN
20969 Ventura Boulevard
Suite 213
Woodland Hills, CA 91364

Art, poetry, and music integrated.

COMMON SENSE PRESS

P.O. Box 1365
8786 Highway 21
Melrose, FL 32666
(904) 475-5757

Learning Language Arts through Literature series, *The Common Sense Reading Program,* first grade skills. *The Great Editing Adventure Series; The Reading Skills Discovery Series, Bookshelf Collections, Math Sense Building Blocks Program, 100 Sheep, Grocery Cart Math, 3 - Way Math Cards,* and *The Wordsmith Series. Creating Books with Children, For the Love of Reading, Frances Study Guide, How to Create Your Own Unit Study, Success With Unit Studies,* and *The Unit Study Idea Book,* by Valerie Bendt. *We Home School,* by Debbie Strayer. *How to Teach Any Child to Spell / Tricks of the Trade,* and *How to Home School.*

CORNERSTONE CURRICULUM PROJECT

2006 Flat Creek
Richardson, TX 75080
(214) 235-5149

Making Math Meaningful, Science the Search, Music and Moments with the Masters, and *Adventures in Art*

CROSSWAY BOOKS

Division of Good News Publishers
Westchester, IL 60153

For the Children's Sake, by Susan Schaeffer Macaulay. *Books Children Love: A Guide to the Best Children's Literature,* by Elizabeth Wilson. *Teaching Children: A Curriculum Guide to What Children Need to Know at Each Level Through Sixth Grade,* by Diane Lopez.

CUISENAIRE CO. OF AMERICA, INC.

12 Church Street
New Rochelle, NY 10801

Cuisenaire Rods and texts.

EDUCATION SERVICES

8825 Blue Mountain Drive
Golden, CA 80403

You Can Teach Your Child Successfully, A Strong Start In Language, An Easy Start in Arithmetic, and *A Home Start in Reading,* all by Ruth Beechick.

Note: New Homeschooling Resources are available. Contact your Common Sense Press dealer for new product information.

EVAN-MOOR CORPORATION
18 Lower Ragsdale Drive
Monterey, CA 93940

How To Make Books With Children. Grades 1-6.

GREENLEAF PRESS
1570 Old La Guardo Road
Lebanon, TN 37087
(615) 449-1617

Great resources for historically based units. *The Greenleaf Guide to Ancient Egypt, Famous Men of Greece, The Greenleaf Guide to Famous Men of Rome, Famous Men of the Middle Ages*, and *The Greenleaf Guide to Famous Men of the Middle Ages.*

HEAR AND LEARN PUBLICATIONS
14516 N.E. 24th Avenue
Vancouver, WA 98686

History Alive Through Music - America, and *History Alive Through Music - Westward Ho!*

HOME RUN ENTERPRISES
12531 Artistocrat Avenue
Garden Grove, CA 92641

Math Mouse Games, Christian Home Education, Curriculum Manual Elementary Grades, and *Christian Home Educators' Curriculum Manual Junior/ Senior High.*

HOMESCHOOLING TODAY
P.O. Box 1425
Melrose, FL 32666
(904) 475-3088

A bi-monthly magazine designed specifically for home-schooling families and those who take an active role in their children's education. Practical, easy-to-understand, and ready-to-use ideas are presented for every age group.

THE LITERACY PRESS
Eunice Coleman
24 Lake Drive
DeBary, FL 32713

Math Literacy with Your One Hundred Board.

THE MOORE FOUNDATION
  Box 1
  Camas, WA 98607
  (206) 835-2736

  Winston Grammar Kit, Math-It, Home Style Teaching, Home Spun Schools, Home Grown Kids, and *The Moore Report.*

NATIONAL GALLERY OF ART
  Washington, D.C. 20565

  Send for fine art print catalog.

NATIONAL GEOGRAPHIC SOCIETY
  Dept. 1675
  Washington, D.C. 20036

  Exploring Your World, the Adventure of Geography.

THE PARADIGM COMPANY
  Box 45161
  Boise, ID 83711

  Alpha-Phonics

SAXON PUBLISHERS, INC.
  1320 West Lindsey
  Norman, OK 73069

  Math textbooks for K through 12th grade.

THE TEACHING HOME
  P.O. Box 20219
  Portland, OR 97220-0219

  A Christian magazine for home educators.